Followership

Followership

What It Takes to Lead

James H. Schindler

BUSINESS EXPERT PRESS

First published in 2015 by
Business Expert Press, LLC
222 East 46th Street, New York, NY 10017
www.businessexpertpress.com

ISBN-13: 978-1-60649-732-6 (paperback)
ISBN-13: 978-1-60649-733-3 (e-book)

Business Expert Press Human Resource Management and Organizational Behavior Collection

Collection ISSN: 1946-5637 (print)
Collection ISSN: 1946-5645 (electronic)

Cover and interior design by Exeter Premedia Services Private Ltd., Chennai, India

First edition: 2015

10 9 8 7 6 5 4 3 2 1

Printed in the United States of America.

Abstract

Followers dominate all organizations, but a preoccupation with leaders hinders the consideration of the importance of followers and the relationship between followers and leaders. The topic of this book is how to become a better leader by becoming a better follower. The book includes chapters on the topics of: leadership theory, followership theory, preparation for the job, understanding what is required for the job, communication, initiative, positive attitude, responsibility, problem solving, and teamwork. This book provides suggestions for becoming an exemplary follower which will demonstrate and manifest the skills associated with leadership and bridge the gap between leadership training and followership.

Keywords

followership, followership theory, leadership, leadership theory, mentoring, success

Contents

Preface

Most books about leadership either do not mention followership at all or just touch lightly on the topic. More often than not leadership books review leadership theories and traits and characteristics of leaders. All of this information is important and worth knowing, but there is more to the leadership equation. This book is about the other side of the equal sign, followership.

Followers usually go unheralded when it comes time to pass out accolades for achieving a difficult goal. But the goal would not have been met if there were no followers doing the work, such as making the sales or whatever the job requires. One of the necessary items required by a leader is exemplary followers to complete the task or goal at hand. Followers dominate all organizations, but a preoccupation with the leader hinders the consideration of the importance of followers and the relationship between followers and leaders. This book is about how to become a better leader by becoming a better follower.

I begin with two introductory chapters, Leadership Theory and Followership Theory. With the foundation laid, I provide a chapter about how to prepare for the job you would like to have and how to improve your performance in your current position. The remaining chapters of the book are to help you understand what is required of you in order to be an exemplary follower. You will learn how to communicate, demonstrate initiative, maintain a positive mental attitude, accept personal responsibility for your actions, learn how to solve problems, and finally you will learn how to determine how you fit within your team, whatever your team may be.

The writing style of this book is lively and easy to read. I kept the technical jargon at a minimum and provided many examples throughout the book to hold the reader's attention. In Chapter 3, I provide tips to help you to prepare for any job or position you intend to have, and to help you understand your personal motivation, I provide a survey as a diagnostic tool. Additionally, I have provided useful suggestions to add to your tool box with chapters that will help you with communication, initiative, positive mental attitude, personal responsibility, problem-solving, and teamwork.

Acknowledgments

Many people have helped me along the way. My sincere thanks to Dr. Richard I. Lester, Dean of Academic Affairs, Ira C. Eaker Center for Professional Development, Air University, Maxwell AFB, AL, who helped me crystallize my thoughts about followership and strengthen my belief of the importance of followership to the leadership process. I would also like to thank Dr. Charlene Dunfee, my DBA dissertation committee chair at Walden University. Dr. Dunfee's guidance and encouragement sparked my initial interest in the need for developing exemplary followers. Finally, I thank my wife Ruthann, for her continued support and encouragement through the writing process.

CHAPTER 1

Introduction to Leadership Theory

Leaders contribute on the average no more than 20 percent to the success of organizations.[1] Those who follow the leader are critical to the completion of the remaining 80 percent. Most people working in organizations, irrespective of their title, spend more time following than leading. Moreover, people tend to move back and forth between leading and following on a continuous basis throughout their working day. Most people follow more than they lead, and following represents 70 to 90 percent of their lives. While people spend most of their working life contributing as followers to the success of their organizations, there is little discussion of what the role of the follower is and how it relates to that of a leader. In most debates about leadership, 80 to 90 percent of people who do the work are never mentioned. We all know that followership dominates organizations; there are many more followers than leaders in any organization you review.[2] So much attention is paid to what makes a person a successful leader, however, this attention ignores the fact that followers are needed by leaders, to get their jobs done.[3]

If you are reading this book, it means you are involved in a continuous search for knowledge and the quest for self-improvement. My intent for this book is to provide a collection of information you most likely have been exposed to in some form or fashion: leadership theory. And to perhaps provide some information that you may not have thought about as of yet: followership theory and how it applies to the practice of leadership. *Followership* is the ability of individuals to follow the instructions of their superior to achieve organizational goals.[4]

Followership is not synonymous with being a subordinate. Ira Chaleff stated that "Followers and leaders both orbit around the purpose, followers do not orbit around the leader."[5] Being a follower is not the same as being a subordinate. You can be one or the other, but an exemplary follower shares a common purpose with the leader. The exemplary follower believes in what the organization is trying to accomplish, wants everyone to succeed, and works tirelessly to make that happen.[6]

Barbara Kellerman said, "Followers are more important to leaders than leaders are to followers." A leader cannot be a leader without any followers. But can a person be both a leader and a follower at the same time? I believe they can and here is why. Think about a simple organizational chart for any company, most likely it will look something like this:

Why is it important to understand that an employee can be both a leader and a follower at the same time? Many times an organizational chart has more than two levels of supervision. We should add at least one additional level to the chart and notice what happens to the followers in the previous chart. Now they have become leaders for the folks below them in the chart and followers of the folks above them in the chart. So it appears there are people in an organization who are both leaders and followers at the same time.

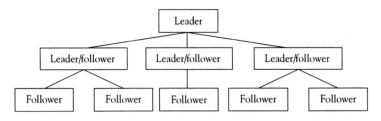

If there are people in an organization that are leaders and followers at the same time, then what do you think has been missing from any of the leadership training you have attended, or any of the leadership books you have read? You are correct, information about how and what it takes to be a good follower. Think back for a moment to your first job as an adult, where were you on the preceding organizational chart? Most likely it was in one of the pure follower spots toward the bottom of the chart. Think about what it took, in that company, to move into one of the leader or follower positions? More than likely, an individual had to do their job in an exemplary fashion in order to be recognized as someone with leadership potential.

This book is not just another self-help leadership book similar to many you have read and studied in the past. This book should help you understand what it takes to be a good follower. I submit that in order to be a good leader you must first be a good follower. Therefore, I want you to know how to be a good follower. That is right; in order to be a good leader you must first be a good follower. All of us at some point either as a child or as an adult, working and making a living for our families, have been a follower.

This word follower can conjure up many images. In can remind one of many things such as the religious followers of Buddha, Mohamed, or Jesus. Alternatively, it can remind us of the hundreds of lemmings running toward cliffs and following the one in front and over the cliff they go. Having grown up in the Midwest my Mother always said that I did not want to be a follower. She always used the lemming example. When I pointed out that my friend Bill got to do such and such, she would reply, "Well if Bill jumped off a cliff would you follow him over the edge?" I still get images of those lemmings rushing over the edge of a cliff when I think of my Mother extolling the fact that I should not be a follower. Although the stories may vary, many of you may have no doubt had the same or similar experience. As a result of that early training, the term follower more often than not has gotten a bad rap. No one wants to be a follower. However, I submit that being a good follower, or being an exemplary follower, is not a bad thing.

I fast forward to the beginnings of my career in the U.S. Air Force. At basic training, every recruit arrived as an individual. However, that changed quickly; each recruit received the same haircut, the same clothes, and, if one wore glasses, the same glasses. We all looked alike; we were not individuals any longer we were members of the group known as a flight. We trained as a flight; we ate together as a flight; we exercised as a flight; and we were rewarded and punished as a flight. The individual differences between us were diminished until we all became as one: one group of real followers. We were taught and trained that we must be good followers. We learned quickly to follow orders exactly, or there would be dire consequences.

Before too long, all of my hard work and nearly constant attention of my drill instructor began to pay off, I learned how to be a good follower. The fruit of this hard work was evidenced by the fact that one day after some very strenuous training I was told to report to my drill instructor's office. There he told me that because of my recognized ability to follow orders and direction (in other words, I was a good follower), I was going to be assigned a leadership position within the flight. He said I was to be assigned as a *squad leader*, I was to become a leader of men. However, all of my training so far had been about following; I had not heard a single thing about leading. How did he know that I had leadership potential? He had only observed me following orders and readily accepting direction. I did not understand how as a good follower I could become a leader. Perhaps a person is both a leader and a follower at the same time.

A while back, I did a Google search for leadership theory. The results were about what I expected; Google searched for 0.30 seconds and returned 48,100,000 hits. Then I searched "followership theory" and the results were not what I expected. Google searched for 0.20 seconds and returned 112,000 hits, less than one quarter of 1 percent of the material had anything to do with followership. I expected more information about followership, after all nearly everyone is a follower of some type, and few are actual leaders. This Google search revealed a great deal of information about leadership theories such as *Great Man* theories, trait theories, contingency theories, behavioral theories, transactional theories, and transformational theories. It is important to gain a clear understanding of these leadership theories in order to better understand how exemplary followership relates to those theories.

Great Man Theory

If we look at the great leaders of the past, we see history often portrays them as heroic and even mythical. These leaders appear to have been destined to rise to positions of leadership when required. Even today, sports heroes, top executives, and politicians are often set apart and, in most instances, thought of as leaders. These people are characterized as natural leaders, born with a set of personal qualities that made them effective leaders. These people are good examples of the Great Man theory, which makes the assumptions that leaders are born and not made and possess certain characteristics which were inherited and that great leaders can arise when there is a great need. The term Great Man was coined by Thomas Carlyle in 1888 because leadership was thought of primarily as a male quality, especially in terms of military leadership.[7] The characteristics that these great leaders were born with have been cited as being paramount to becoming an effective leader. The study of these characteristics began the interest of trying to come to an understanding of what leadership is and, as a result, researchers have focused on the leader. At the genesis, researchers focused on the traits that some people inherit leading to trait theories.

Trait Theories

According to the trait theorists, people inherit traits and qualities that make some better suited to lead than others. The early trait theories attempted to identify specific behavioral and personality characteristics shared by leaders. Once they identified some of these leadership characteristics, the researchers had a difficult time explaining how some people who exhibited these traits were not also leaders. Researchers started coming up with personality traits. Gordon Allport[8] came up with a list of 4,000 personality traits; Raymond Cattell[9] came up with 16 personality traits; and Hans Eysenck[10] developed only a three-factor theory.

Most researchers, today, have settled down with five basic dimensions of personality. The body of evidence of this theory has been growing beginning with the research of D.W. Fiske[11] and later expanded upon by other researchers including Norman[12], Goldberg[13], and McCrae and Costa.[14] Researchers today believe that these models were either too complex or too simplistic and, as a result, a five-trait theory has emerged to describe the basic personality traits of human personality.

These five-core personality traits are broad categories of personality traits and are known as the *big five*. Ernest Tupes and Raymond Christal advanced the initial model in 1961.[15] Many times researchers do not agree on the labels but here is my version:

1. *Extraversion:* This trait includes characteristics such as excitability, sociability, talkativeness, assertiveness, and high amounts of emotional expressiveness.

2. *Agreeableness:* This personality dimension includes attributes such as trust, altruism, kindness, affection, and other prosocial behaviors.

3. *Conscientiousness:* Common features of this dimension include high levels of thoughtfulness, with good impulse control and goal-directed behaviors. Those high in conscientiousness tend to be organized and mindful of details.

4. *Neuroticism:* Individuals high in this trait tend to experience emotional instability, anxiety, moodiness, irritability, and sadness.

5. *Openness:* This trait features characteristics such as imagination and insight, and those high in this trait also tend to have a broad range of interests.

Contingency Theories

Next are contingency theories of leadership. These theories focus on particular variables related to the situation that might determine which particular style of leadership is best suited. In the early 60s, Fred Fielder advanced the first theory using the contingency approach, the *contingency theory of effectiveness.* The central idea of this early theory is that leadership effectiveness (in terms of group performance) depends on the interaction of two factors: the leader's job or motivations and aspects of the situation.[16] The work of Fielder and many colleagues are considered as classic contributions to the body of knowledge about person and situational aspects of leadership.

Path–goal theory was originally developed by Martin Evans in 1970 and expanded by Robert House in 1971 into a more complex contingency theory.[17] Drawing on expectancy theory, House suggested that a leader should help elucidate the path for followers to achieve group goals. This involves the leader employing particular behaviors in specific situations to increase follower satisfaction and motivate efforts toward task accomplishment. The theory identifies four types of leader behavior that include supportive (relations oriented), directive (task-oriented), achievement oriented, and participative leader performance, as well as two aspects of the situation, namely, follower characteristics and job characteristics.[18]

The normative decision model, originally developed by Victor Vroom and Phillip Yetton in 1973 and later revised by Victor Vroom and Arthur Jago, emphasizes situational factors more than leadership behaviors.[19] It outlines a set of five different decision-making strategies that range on a continuum from directive to participative decision making. These strategies include two types of autocratic styles (the leader decides alone), two types of consultative styles (the leader consults followers, but decides alone), and a group decision-making option (group consensus).[20]

The final contingency theory in this section is the situational leadership theory put forth by Paul Hersey and Ken Blanchard in 1969.[21] This theory proposes that leadership effectiveness depends on the leader's ability to tailor his or her behavior to the demands of the situation, namely, the subordinate's level of maturity. Hersey and Blanchard highlight four different types of leadership behavior based on combining directive and supportive behavior: telling (high directive, low support), selling (high directive, high supporting), participating (low directive, high supportive), and delegating (low directive, low supportive).[22]

Behavioral Theories

Behavioral theories of leadership are based upon the belief that great leaders are made, not born.[23] Rooted in behaviorism, this leadership theory focuses on the actions of leaders, not on mental qualities or internal states. According to this theory, people can *learn* to become leaders through teaching and observation. Behavioral theory promotes the value of leadership styles with an emphasis on concern for people and collaboration. It promotes participative decision making and team development by supporting individual needs and aligning individual and group objectives. Behavioral theories of leadership, also known as "the style approach to leadership" focuses on the behavior of the leader and what leaders do and how they act.[24]

Transactional Theory

Management theories, also known as transactional theories, focus on the role of supervision, organization, and group performance.[25] These theories base leadership on a system of rewards and punishments. In business, managerial theories are used when employees are successful, and they are rewarded; when they fail, they are reprimanded or punished. Transactional leadership involves motivating and directing followers primarily through appealing to their own self-interest.[26] The power of transactional leaders comes from their formal authority and responsibility in the organization. The main goal of the follower is to obey the instructions of the leader.

The leader believes in motivating through a system of rewards and punishment. If a subordinate does what is desired, a reward will follow, and if he does not go as per the wishes of the leader, a punishment will follow. Here, the exchange between leader and follower takes place to achieve routine performance goals. These exchanges involve four dimensions:[27]

- *Contingent rewards:* Transactional leaders link the goal to rewards, clarify expectations, provide necessary resources, set mutually agreed upon goals, and provides various kinds of rewards for successful performance. They set SMART (specific, measurable, attainable, realistic, and timely) goals for their subordinates.
- *Active management by exception:* Transactional leaders actively monitor the work of their subordinates, watch for deviations from rules and standards, and taking corrective action to prevent mistakes.
- *Passive management by exception:* Transactional leaders only intervene when standards are not met or when the performance is not as per the expectations. They may even use punishment as a response to unacceptable performance.
- *Laissez-faire:* The leader provides an environment where the subordinates get many opportunities to make decisions. The leader himself abdicates responsibilities and avoids making decisions and, therefore, the group often lacks direction.

Transformational Theory

Transformational theories focus upon the connections formed between leaders and followers.[28] Transformational leaders motivate and inspire people by helping group members see the importance and higher good of the task. These leaders are focused on the performance of group members, but also want each person to fulfill his or her potential. Leaders with this style often have high ethical and moral standards. At all levels of the organization—teams, departments, divisions, and organization as a whole—one can find transformational leadership.[29] Such leaders are visionary, inspiring, daring risk-takers, and thoughtful thinkers. They have a charismatic appeal. However, charisma alone is insufficient for changing the way an organization operates. For bringing major changes, transformational leaders must exhibit the following four factors:[30]

- *Inspirational motivation:* The foundation of transformational leadership is the promotion of consistent vision, mission, and a set of values to the members. Their vision is so compelling that they know what they want from every interaction. Transformational leaders guide followers by providing them with a sense of meaning and challenge. They work enthusiastically and optimistically to foster a spirit of teamwork and commitment.
- *Intellectual stimulation:* Such leaders encourage their followers to be innovative and creative. They encourage new ideas from their followers and never criticize them publicly for the mistakes committed by them. The leaders focus on the *what* in problems and do not focus on the blaming part of it. They have no hesitation in discarding an old practice set by them if it is found ineffective.
- *Idealized influence:* They believe in the philosophy that a leader can influence followers only when he practices what he preaches. The leaders act as role models that followers seek to emulate. Such leaders always win the trust and respect of their followers through their action. They typically place their followers' needs over their own, sacrifice their personal gains

for them, and demonstrate high standards of ethical conduct. The use of power by such leaders is aimed at influencing their followers to strive for the common goals of the organization.

- *Individualized consideration:* Leaders serve as mentors to their followers and reward them for creativity and innovation. The followers are treated differently according to their talents and knowledge. Leaders are empowered to make decisions, and they are always provided with the needed support to implement decisions they make.

This chapter has provided a quick review of some of the most important leadership theories. You have reviewed Great Man theories, trait theories, contingency theories, behavioral theories, transactional theories, and transformational theories. The next chapter will provide a brief explanation of followership theories. However, before you get there keep this one critical bit of information somewhere in the back of your mind. Sir Thomas Heath wrote *The Elements of Euclid* in 1908. There he provided one of Euclid's Common Notions—CN-1: Things that are equal to the same thing are also equal to one another.[31] In other words, if A is equal to B and C is equal to B, then A and C are equal to each other. In my mind, this can also mean that if there are certain traits that an effective leader possesses that are the same as certain traits that an exemplary follower possesses, then we can come to the logical conclusion that good leadership and exemplary followership are equal.

Now what about followership theory, where did it come from? Most likely, you have not studied much about followership theory. Why? The reason is clear as a bell; there is not much research about followership and its relationship with leadership. I plan to make that relationship very clear with the remaining chapters of this book. We will begin the remainder of this journey by sharing some information about followership theories. Next we will discuss how to gain an understanding of what is required of you in any job that you may have, now or in the future. Then touch on the need for good communication, the display of initiative, and the need for maintaining a positive mental attitude. Then we will proceed to a discussion of what it means to accept responsibility for the things you can control. Finally, we will wrap up with a few words about problem solving and teamwork. Both are very important to an exemplary follower.

CHAPTER 2

Followership Theory

What does it mean to be a good follower? Well, as I mentioned in Chapter 1, being a good follower does not mean to follow other lemmings as they run headlong toward the cliff and jump off. The following definition draws on the thoughts of Kelley, a major contributor to the literature on the role of the follower:

> A follower is one who pursues a course of action in common with a leader to achieve an organizational goal. Effective followers make an active decision to contribute towards the achievement of the goal and demonstrate enthusiasm, intelligence, self-reliance and the ability to work with others in pursuit of the goal. Effective followers recognize the authority of the leader and limitations this imposes on their own actions, consider all issues on their merits, make their own decisions, hold their own values, speak their minds and hold themselves accountable for the consequences for their actions.[1]

In other words, active followers, given the necessary information and room to move, can be trusted to take independent action to achieve a particular objective. This action is subject to receiving ongoing assistance and support to resolve issues beyond their spheres of competence and influence, and to receiving recognition for the work they are doing. It is important to note that while the behavior of effective followers may be seen to be simply doing as they are told, their actions are the result of independent thought and decision making and would have been the same in the absence of direction from the leader.

There are a number of activities within various institutions that provide a clear example of how exemplary followers can make a significant difference in the outcome of organized efforts.[2] The traditional fields of religion, military, politics, and team sports are organizations that have followership as the cornerstone of their foundation.[3] Within these organizations, successful followership is built upon the following:

- Belief in the organization's mission, vision, or purpose
- Willingness to subjugate personal interest for the greater good
- Loyalty
- Unity of focus

Efforts to help integrate these concepts into your efforts on behalf of your organization will further enhance your contribution to the success of the organization, and in turn improve your capabilities.

But the preoccupation with the importance of leadership and the leader to that organization has dominated the research and writings on the subject, and hampered research on followership theory. Four interrelated factors have contributed to this lack of research.[4] First, the term followership is nearly always associated with a negative point of view. Followership almost always is presented as a character trait to avoid if one aspires to lead. Second, the traditional hierarchical relationship between leaders and their followers has distorted the effectiveness of the leader and follower exchange. Third, when have you heard of any leadership development program that devotes time to developing an active follower culture and the followership skills that go along with it? Finally, academic business programs have been slow in documenting how characteristics and traits of effective followers parallel the characteristics and traits of effective leaders.

However, followership theory has two main sources: Kelley[5] has provided categories of followers based on traits and attributes and Chaleff[6] describes followers in terms of different behaviors.[7] Arguably, Robert E. Kelley helped to begin the shift in thinking about leadership research and training with his 1988 *Harvard Business Review* article, "In Praise of Followers."[8] Kelley's early research about followership determined there are two basic dimensions that define the way people follow.[9] These dimensions are

1. Do they think for themselves? Are they independent critical thinkers? Or do they look to the leader to do the thinking for them.

2. Are they actively engaged in creating positive energy for the organization? Or is there negative or passive involvement?

From these two dimensions, Kelley derived the five basic styles of followership:[10]

> *The sheep.* Sheep are passive and want a leader to do all the thinking for them, and they also want a leader to motivate them. If you are the boss and you are thinking about what you are going to get your workers to do and how you are going to do that, then you are dealing with sheep.
>
> *The yes-people.* The yes-people are just that; they are always on the leader's side, but they still want the leader to do the thinking and provide them the vision. If the boss asks yes-people to do something, yes-people will go forward and get it done. When they finish the task, they ask, "What do you want me to do next?" Yes-people will put a positive spin on their actions by saying, "I am a doer; that is my job. The boss gets paid to think, and I am a guy who gets the work done." But you know there is more to it than simply doing the job.
>
> *The alienated.* Alienated followers can think for themselves but are negative in nature. If the leaders try to move forward they are the ones that have many reasons why it will not work. They do not try to come up with a solution, but they are cynical about the current plan of action. The alienated see themselves as mavericks, the only ones who have the guts to make a stand.
>
> *The pragmatics.* Pragmatics sit on the fence and see which way the wind is blowing. Once they know the wind direction they get on board, but they will not let the leader pull out of the station without them. They perceive themselves as the status quo. They do what they must to survive, but wait it out until the storms of change blow over.
>
> *The star followers.* Star followers think for themselves and have very positive energy. They give the leader's decisions an independent evaluation, and if they agree, they give full support. If they disagree, they offer constructive alternatives that will help the leader, the organization, or both. Many view these star followers as "leaders in

disguise."[11] Star followers are also often referred to as the right-hand person or the go-to person, and this is where you come into the picture. You should be striving to be that person who gets the job done without involving the boss; you should be making their job easy.

Ira Chaleef[12] developed four dimensions of followership to apply within an organization or group and the fifth dimension for outside the organization or group. Chaleef considered these five behaviors—responsibility, service, challenge, transformation, and leaving—as the five dimensions of courageous followership:[13]

> *The courage to assume responsibility.* These followers do not hesitate to assume responsibility for themselves and the organization. They do not maintain the paternalistic view of the leader. These followers work toward creating opportunities that will allow them to fulfill their potential and maximize their value to the organization.
>
> *The courage to serve.* Followers should not be afraid of the hard work required to serve the leader. Followers who display this dimension readily assume new or additional responsibilities to lighten the load of the leader and help the organization.
>
> *The courage to challenge.* Followers who display this dimension of followership do not hesitate to speak up when the behaviors or policies of the leader conflict with their sense of right and wrong. These individuals are willing to stand out and risk rejection in order to bring issues to light. These followers value organizational harmony and their relationship with the leader but not at the expense of their integrity.
>
> *The courage to participate in the transformation.* The followers who apply this dimension champion the need for change and are willing to stay the course while struggling with the difficulty of real change.
>
> *The courage to take moral action.* Now comes the tough part of Chaleff's[14] proposition. The followers know when it is time to take a stand that differs from the leaders. This stand may be refusing a direct order, appealing to a higher authority, or even resigning. These moral actions require a great deal of courage and involve personal risk.

We have looked briefly at theories that seek to explain the relationship between leaders and followers and the characteristics and attributes associated with good followership. There are plausible follower competencies and components and they are as follows:[15]

- Displays loyalty by showing a deep commitment to the organization, adheres to the vision and priorities of the organization, aligns personal and organizational goals, and disagrees agreeably.
- Functions well in change-oriented environments by serving as a change agent while moving fluidly between the roles of follower and leader.
- Functions well on teams by collaborating, sharing credit, and acting responsibly toward others.
- Demonstrates the ability to think independently and critically by dissenting courageously, takes the initiative, and practices self-management.
- Considers integrity of paramount importance by remaining trustworthy, tells the truth, admits mistakes, and maintains the highest performance standards.

Blackshear pointed out that there should be a new way of looking at followership.[16] Her followership continuum is a development model that focuses on productivity in the workplace as it provides a gauge for measuring and developing employee performance output. The followership continuum is based on the concept that your performance is not constant. For example, your performance may be excellent for one particular supervisor and less than sterling for another. The followership continuum is represented by five stages of dynamic followership performance, presented in the following table:[17]

Followership continuum

Employee	Committed follower	Engaged follower	Effective follower	Exemplary follower
Stage 1	Stage 2	Stage 3	Stage 4	Stage 5

Stage 1 employee is the stage of followership within the workplace that begins by becoming an employee. A stage 2 committed follower on the continuum is characterized by the employee becoming bound to the mission, idea, or organization. A stage 3 engaged follower is an active supporter willing to go above and beyond the routine. A stage 4 effective follower is considered capable and dependable along with all of the previous characteristics. The stage 5 exemplary follower could easily be the leader. The exemplary follower, however, sets ego aside and works to support the leader by leading themselves. Where do you fit along the followership continuum?

As you have read the theories and concepts presented in the chapter, it is important to determine what to do with this knowledge. In other words, how does one become a good follower? Followership is an important portion of leadership, perhaps more important than leadership styles, skills, and theories. For we all know, without any followers there are no leaders. Colonel Phillip S. Mellinger states that "If we can master this task [being a good follower], and master it well, then we will, in turn, be better leaders when the challenge confronts us. We must learn to follow before we can learn to lead."[18] Mellinger has some very good tips and rules for followers in order to become that exemplary follower:[19]

1. Don't blame your boss for an unpopular decision or policy; it is your job to support, not undermine.
2. Disagree with your boss if necessary, but do it in private, avoid embarrassing situations, and never reveal to others what was discussed.
3. Make a decision, and then run it past the boss; use your initiative.
4. Accept responsibility whenever it is offered.
5. Tell the truth and do not quibble; your boss will be giving advice based upon what you said.
6. Do your homework; give your boss all the information necessary to make a decision.
7. When making a recommendation, keep in mind you are most likely the person who will have to implement the recommendation. This means you must know your own limitations and weaknesses, as well as your strengths.

8. Keep your boss informed of what's going on in the organization; people will be reluctant to tell him or her of their problems and successes. You should do that for them, and assume someone else will tell the boss about yours.

9. If you find a problem, fix it. Don't worry about who will get the blame or who now gets the praise.

10. Put in more than an honest day's work, but don't ever forget the needs of your family. If they are unhappy, you will be too, and your job performance will suffer accordingly.

This all sounds pretty good. But what does it mean to you in your particular situation? What does your boss expect of you in order for you to become a good follower? According to the former CEO of Honeywell, there are seven responsibilities you need to cover.[20] First, you need to get involved, make sure you are involved in the day to day functions of your particular situation. Second, generate ideas; this is one way to get involved. If you are innovative and creative and willing to share those ideas, it will demonstrate a commitment to the organization. Third, you should collaborate with your peers and others and not resist the sharing of credit. There is an old saying that goes something like this, "It is amazing how much work can get done if it does not matter who gets the credit." Next is, confront reality. It is necessary to face up to the realities of the organization and decide if any adjustments need to be made. You should be willing to change your position in the face of new facts. Fifth, you must be willing to risk failure. You will need to look at problem solving and try to come up with a new solution. In other words, from the preceding list involve number two. If the solution works, great, but if it fails, then learn from it and continue to move forward. But you must be willing to risk that failure or nothing will get accomplished. Sixth, you need to show some initiative. Develop and implement a plan of action. And finally, develop your leadership capability. If you work on all of the aforementioned six tasks and master them to some degree, you will naturally be working on your leadership capacity.

Remember my earlier basic training story? I became identified as a potential leader by merely doing my job well. As the result of me having accepted the responsibility to become as good as I possibly could at the task at hand, I was recognized as a potential leader. Going forward in this book, I will provide a unique perspective from which you can view leadership and followership and perhaps infuse the concepts covered into your career progression plan, and become identified as someone with leadership potential within your organization.

CHAPTER 3

Preparation for the Job

The first two chapters were a review of leadership theories and an exposure to followership theory. Keep in mind that we also looked at the characteristics of leaders and the characteristics of good followers. As a result of this unique perspective of leadership and followership, you are coming to the important part of this book. The rest of the book deals with how to be an exemplary follower and, therefore, an extraordinary leader. Keep in mind as you read the remainder of this book Euclid's common notion one—CN-1: Things which are equal to the same thing are also equal to one another.[1] First, we need to discuss just what is your job?

What Is Your Job?

Whether you are a new hire, or you have been on the job for quite some time, it is important for you to know what your job is. What were you hired to do for the organization that hired you? What is your job?

I submit to you that your job is to make your boss's job easy. Rachelle J. Canter, author of *Make the Right Career Move*, suggests that you become invaluable to the boss so that you are the default go-to-person. If you are competent in your job, if you do the best you can on each assignment, you make your boss's job easy; because, they do not have to accomplish the task themselves, they can count on you to do it correctly.

"Anticipate (the boss') needs" Canter says, "The difference between good employees and excellent employees is that the latter do not just comply with requests well, they anticipate needs of their bosses and deliver above and beyond what the boss expects."[2] Once again, you are making the boss's job easy as you think ahead and anticipate what might be coming next.

To get to that point, you need to be direct, and that means being prepared to ask the right questions. Canter recommends, "When you do something, check in with the boss to ensure that you helped him or her out—don't assume you did."[3] Ask the boss for feedback about how the project you completed turned out. Did it provide the necessary answers? Did it help prepare for the presentation?

"You are not the boss, but you are a reflection of your boss, and it behooves you both to project a positive image," says Elizabeth Freedman.[4] "It is like the old Vidal Sassoon commercial—if you do not look good, your boss does not look good," she says. And that idea extends beyond having your shirt tucked in, and your pants ironed. "Make sure anything that represents the team—whether it is an e-mail or voice mail coming from you—also reflects you and the boss in a professional, polished way."[5] Remember that what you do and how you do it reflects on your boss.

Competency

You must, at least, be competent in your profession. To be competent means: having suitable or sufficient skill, knowledge, experience, and so forth for some purpose; suitably qualified.[6] How do you become competent? That will depend upon your profession; you may need extra schooling or specialized training. Whatever the case, you need to know as much as you can about the techniques, processes, and policies involved in your job. Frontline managers, though, instinctively feel that competence is something more than a list of attributes. They sense that a person's way of seeing work is just as important; competent workers have a particular vision of what their work is and why it is that way.[7] You will need to develop a clear vision of what you want in your career in future. Without a vision you'll run around in circles; waste your precious time, energy, and other resources; and be subject to disappointment and failure.[8]

Motivation

For our purposes, we will take a look at work motivation and achievement motivation. Work motivation "is a set of energetic forces that originate both within as well as beyond an individual's being, to initiate work-related behavior, and to determine its form, direction, intensity, and duration."[9] Achievement motivation can be broken down into three types:

- *Achievement*—seeks position advancement, feedback, and a sense of accomplishment
- *Authority*—need to lead, make an impact, and be heard by others
- *Affiliation*—need for friendly social interactions and to be liked.

Because most individuals have a combination of these three types (in various proportions), an understanding of these achievement motivation characteristics can be a useful assistance to management in job placement, recruitment, and so forth.[10] The need for achievement theory is in many ways similar to the need for mastery and self-actualization in Maslow's hierarchy of needs and growth in the Existence, Relatedness, and Growth (ERG) theory. By applying this theory, we can see that individuals strive to achieve their goals and grow within the organization.[11] These employees tend to be dedicated to their work and strive hard to succeed; they also demonstrate a strong desire for increasing their knowledge and for feedback on their performance, often in the form of performance appraisal.

Here are a few things I would recommend you do.

1. Learn what information your boss likes to see and get it to him or her before it is requested.[12] Never make your boss chase data that you can proactively provide.

   - When employees know the boss is looking for certain information, many times, instead of proactively providing the data, they merely wait until their boss contacts them multiple times. The boss is asking for the same data week after week, and you obediently gather the data and provide it to the boss. There is an easy way to simplify life for your boss and separate yourself from your peers. Just do it without waiting to be told.

2. Learn how your boss likes to see reports, metrics, and so forth.[13]

   - What format does your boss use when providing updates to his superior? PDF docs, digital power points, excel spreadsheets, and so forth. If you use the same form, you can simplify your boss's life by speeding up the process of using your data in his or her reports.

- Does your boss favor one graph over another? I can tell you from experience, the higher up your boss is, the more particular he will be.
- Does your boss favor summary reports and only look at the details as a last resort or does your boss always dig into the details? This makes a big difference in how you should package and deliver your information. Any time you present to another person or group, you should always know your audience and structure your presentation to their liking. This is even more important when your boss is in the room.

3. Be proactive in your management style.[14]

- Your boss should not have to identify mistakes in your organization and push you to resolve them. You should always be looking further ahead than your boss. If your boss wants a report once a week, create your own report and schedule it to run every day or two. Then make sure you are addressing any issue before hand. (You should be doing this on your own but, at a minimum, make sure you are always ahead of the needs of your boss.)

4. When it comes to meetings, you need to make an effort and do the work.[15]

- Never make your boss manage your schedule. Make an effort to schedule the meetings if you can.
- Never double book your boss's calendar without speaking to him.
- If you have to schedule a meeting at short notice, follow up with your boss and make sure the time works for him. You should always assume your boss is busier than you are. It does not matter if your boss plays solitaire all day. The boss is the boss, and until you get promoted above him, your boss needs to be treated as the boss.

- What is the best time to present reports to your boss? Is your boss a morning person or does your boss hate the world before 10 a.m.? You should pay attention to this. It will make a difference. If your boss is happiest in the morning, that is the time to schedule your budget meeting.

5. Try to settle issues between coworkers directly. Don't turn your boss into a "work parent" breaking up fights between two children.[16]

6. Whatever you do, make sure it makes your boss look good to his boss.[17] Unless you are just looking for a fight to take your boss's job, your best bet for promotion and raise is making sure your work reflects well on your boss. Few people want to promote someone who just backstabbed the last guy. They are looking for someone who will be dedicated to them, and your past actions say more about you than any interview will.

I cannot stress enough the last point. You prepare for your next promotion by making sure you are doing all that you can to get your boss promoted. Now this does not mean you should spend your entire career kissing your boss's back side? No, there is a big difference in doing your job efficiently, so it makes your boss's life and job easier and spending your days telling your boss how good he looks in his new car.[18]

Here is an exercise to help you pinpoint the origins of your motivation. The following is reprinted with permission from *Motivating Yourself for Achievement* by Arthur Bell and Dale Smith.[19]

Directions: Read each question carefully. Select the answer that matches your feelings. (In some cases, neither answer will fit your feelings precisely. In those cases, choose the answer that comes closer than the other answer to your feelings.) When you have completed the assessment, transfer your answers to the answer sheet at the end of the assessment. There you will also find an interpretation of your scores.

1. You have a major exam coming up as part of your college study or work life. Which would be more effective in motivating you to study?

    a. Encouragement from your professor or boss

    b. Your ambition

2. A new job has opened up in your company. You are deciding whether or not to apply for it. Which would be more effective in motivating you to apply?

    a. Information from the company assuring you that all applicants have a fair chance.

    b. Your own ideas about where this new job could lead you on your upward career path.

3. You are trying to decide whether to rent an attractive apartment at a rental rate that is significantly higher than you are now paying. Which would be more effective in motivating you to rent an apartment?

    a. Your confidence in yourself and your financial future.

    b. Moral support from friends and relatives who would like to see you living in a nicer place.

4. You are working on a project along with four other people. A looming deadline requires that you work on Saturday without additional compensation. Which would be more effective in motivating you to work on the Saturday?

    a. Your ideas that the boss will take note of this extra effort and reward you in some way in the future.

    b. The fact that the other four people on the project have agreed to work on Saturday.

5. You are contemplating a change in careers. Which would be more effective in motivating you to make a change?

    a. Advice from those who know you and your abilities best, including a favorite college professor.

    b. Your belief that a career change would make work more interesting and rewarding for you.

6. Three people in your work group received a raise this year, and three did not. You were one of the ones who did not. You are deciding whether or not to talk with your boss about this situation. Which would be more effective in motivating you to talk with your boss?

    a. The rumor that your performance appraisal was just as good as those of the people who received the raise.

    b. Your idea that making the boss aware of your negative feelings about the situation will encourage him to give you a raise sooner rather than later.

7. Your company's sports team wants you to join. You do not feel that you are a particularly good player. Which would be more effective in motivating you to join the team?

    a. Your willingness to accept new challenges and try new experiences.

    b. Friendly invitations and encouragement from several members of the team who really want you to join.

8. You are shopping for a new car. A sales person has stated a price, and you are deciding whether or not to buy. Which would be more effective in motivating you to buy the car?

    a. Your expectation that you could not find the car cheaper elsewhere.

    b. Your knowledge that two of your friends bought the same car model for the same price within the last few weeks.

9. Your boss tells you that you have been asked to speak for the company at an upcoming convention. Which would be more effective in motivating you to accept this speaking invitation?

    a. Your boss's statement that you could be making a big contribution to the company as a speaker.

    b. Your confidence that you could represent the company well as a speaker.

10. Economic conditions have forced your company to consider pay cutbacks for all workers. Which would be more effective in motivating you to accept a pay cut?

    a. The knowledge that all workers are receiving the same percentage of cut in their pay.

    b. Your belief that your company will appreciate your willingness to accept a pay cut and will reward you when better times return.

11. You are trying to decide where to go on vacation. Which would be more effective in motivating you to select a particular location?

    a. Your long-term desire to see that part of the world.

    b. Reports from friends who have returned recently from that region.

12. One of your friends complains to you that she is not getting ahead in her job as quickly as she would like. Which one of these approaches would you use in motivating her to talk to her employer about the problem?

    a. You urge her to assemble proof that other workers in her group with less skill and experience have been moved ahead more quickly that she has.

    b. You urge her to put together work materials to show how valuable she can be to the company in a more advanced position.

13. Due to circumstances beyond your control, you have to turn in a term paper late. You are worried the professor will not accept the paper. Which would be more effective in motivating you to talk with the professor about the problem?

    a. Advice from another classmate who had the same professor last term.

    b. Your belief that the professor will be reasonable in understanding the circumstances.

14. Parking spots are hard to find at your workplace. An assigned parking place close to the building is highly prized. You have waited for such a place for more than two years. However, when a prime spot becomes available, it was given to an employee who had not been with the company as long as you had. You are deciding whether or not to complain to senior management. Which would be more effective in motivating you to complain about the problem?

   a. The lack of fairness involved in passing you over for a more junior employee.
   b. The influence this slight will have on your morale and productivity in the company in the future.

15. You are deciding whether or not to join a community college class to learn a foreign language. Which would be more effective in motivating you to join the class?

   a. Your desire to learn the language.
   b. The fact that two of your friends are already in the class and like it very much.

16. You have just graduated from college and have no particular job prospects. Which would be more effective in motivating you to search the job ads in the newspaper?

   a. Your hope of finding a position that interests you.
   b. Your idea that not finding a position would be a waste of the effort and expense you put into college.

17. You are trying to read in the library. Two librarians are talking loudly a short distance from you. Which would be more effective in motivating you to ask the librarians to talk more quietly?

   a. The sign posted near the library door: "Please maintain QUIET in the library."
   b. Your growing irritation at being unable to concentrate on your reading due to the librarians' chatter.

18. Your elderly parents are drawing up their wills, with financial provisions for you and your younger brother. Your parents ask you in private whether you would like to inherit their life insurance (a fixed amount) or their stocks, which could rise or fall in value in the period prior to their deaths. What motivates us to select the stocks?

   a. If you do receive substantially more that your brother (who will receive the life insurance), you can point out that you took the risk that the stocks could have gone down.
   b. The stocks have a chance of becoming much more valuable than they are at present.

19. You must decide whether to spend money for new clothes for an upcoming business trip. Which is more effective in motivating your decision?

   a. It's been a while since you bought new clothes, and you feel you deserve them.
   b. Several work associates who will accompany you on the trip already have told you about their plans to buy new clothes.

20. Contrary to the usual policy of allowing managers to use company cars for entertaining clients, the new policy prohibits the use of company cars in this way for all employees below the vice president level. You are not yet a vice president. Which would you be motivated to do?

   a. Accept the new policy without complaint because you hope you will soon be named vice president of the company.
   b. Accept the new policy without complaint because it applies equally to everyone at your level.

21. A good friend has recently lost her job. Which approach would you tend to use in encouraging the friend to seek another job?

   a. Gather the help-wanted ads that might be suitable for your friend.
   b. Tell your friend how valuable her talents are.

22. Membership at the company gym is determined by drawing because many more employees sought membership than the gym could accommodate. Which would be more effective in motivating you to enter your name in the drawing?

    a. The idea that all employees have the same chance, assuming the drawing is fair.

    b. Your expectation that you might get lucky and be drawn as a new gym member.

23. The grass around your home desperately needs to be mowed. Which would be more effective in motivating you to do the job yourself?

    a. You know you have the strength and equipment to do the job.

    b. You have seen many of your neighbors mowing their own grass.

24. At the circus, you are deciding whether or not to pay a dollar for a chance to knock down three milk bottles with a softball and win a prize. You end up deciding not to do so. Which is more effective in determining your decision?

    a. You are not sure you throw a softball well enough to hit the bottle.

    b. You suspect the milk bottles have been weighted so they will not fall easily.

25. You have the opportunity to buy stock in a promising new company. Which would be more effective in determining your decision?

    a. The optimistic attitudes of two of your friends who also are investing in the company.

    b. Your ability to take reasonable risks, for better or for worse.

26. You have tickets to attend the theater. However, you are disappointed when a famous actor scheduled to play the lead role fails to show up. His understudy takes over, and the show goes on. Which is the main source of your disappointment?

a. On other evenings, theatergoers paid the same price for tickets and saw the famous actor, not the understudy.

b. You had looked forward to seeing the famous actor perform.

27. You are trying to decide whether or not to return to college to earn an additional degree. Which would be more effective in motivating you to do so?

a. Your desire to learn more, and your confidence in your abilities.

b. Stories from your friends about how much they enjoyed returning to college

28. You have worked hard and well for the company for more than a year—but so far without a raise. Which would be more likely to motivate you to expect a raise in the near future?

a. The boss knows you have been expecting a raise and you aren't willing to wait much longer without quitting.

b. The company has a history of rewarding good performance sooner or later.

29. You are shopping for a ring. Which would be more effective in motivating you to buy one?

a. The jeweler's assurance that you are buying a quality ring at a deeply discounted price.

b. Your own good shopping sense if you find the right ring.

30. After five years with the company, you and nine other workers each receive a small pin at a luncheon in your honor. Which would be your likely reaction?

a. Satisfaction, because all workers who had worked for the company for five years received the same pin.

b. Dissatisfaction, because you were an outstanding worker, and you expected the company to present you with something more substantial than a pin after five years.

Scoring

Place checks for your a or b choices in the following columns:

Total the checks in each column and place the number in the space provided.

1. a _____ b_____   2. a _____ b_____
3. a _____ b_____   4. a _____ b_____
5. a _____ b_____   6. a _____ b_____
7. a _____ b_____   8. a _____ b_____
9. a _____ b_____   10. a _____ b_____
11. a _____ b_____   12. a _____ b_____
13. a _____ b_____   14. a _____ b_____
15. a _____ b_____   16. a _____ b_____
17. a _____ b_____   18. a _____ b_____
19. a _____ b_____   20. a _____ b_____
21. a _____ b_____   22. a _____ b_____
23. a _____ b_____   24. a _____ b_____
25. a _____ b_____   26. a _____ b_____
27. a _____ b_____   28. a _____ b_____
29. a _____ b_____   30. a _____ b_____

_____ _____   _____ _____

O   I   F   E

Interpretation

The higher your score in any column, the dominant that tendency is in your approach to self-motivation.

> *O-outside motivators.* If your score is higher in the O column than in the I column, you tend to pay more attention to what others say and feel as a motivational influence. On the positive side, your knowledge of this tendency can make you aware of the advice, comments, feedback, and guidance provided by others. You tend to, after all, find this information crucial to your motivation and decision making. Know it accurately and extensively can help you find powerful

motivators. On the other hand, you might want to guard against too complete a reliance on the opinions of others to the exclusion of knowing your own mind and heart. A high-tendency score in the column also could be your warning to think hard about what you think, want, feel, and need.

I-inside motivators. If your score is higher in the I column than in the O column, you tend to find your motivation more in your own thought and feelings than in what others think and feel. Your high score can indicate the positive influence of knowing who you are and what you want. You are able on most occasions to shut out the distracting and conflicting opinions and advice of the outside world so you can hear your own authentic intentions and perspective. On the other hand, a tendency to shut out the world can be hazardous if practiced too rigidly. A high score in this column might alert you to a tendency to discount all opinions other than your own. You might want to listen not only to your own inner voice but also to the outside voices that you respect.

F-fairness. If you score higher in the F column than in the E column, you tend to be motivated more by a sense of fairness than by your expectation for what might occur. A high score in this column indicates that you are *moved* (i.e., motivated) by equity in human affairs. When you feel you or someone else has been treated unjustly, you are energized to action. In the great scheme of things, this sensitivity to fairness is no doubt admirable. However, if you focus only on the fairness of a notoriously unfair world, you might find yourself enmeshed within endless efforts to make things right instead of making things move forward. For example, your aversion to instances of unfairness in a large corporation could involve all your energies in an effort to correct the situation. Although such a crusade is undoubtedly noble, it often might take the place of other worthwhile goals you could be pursuing.

E-expectations. If your score is higher in the E column than in the F column, you tend to be motivated more by what you expect or hope will happen rather than by what you feel is fair or deserved. A high score in the column indicates that you tend to be motivated by *blue sky*, that is, the endless possibilities for the future.

This optimism for what lies ahead is a wonderful quality, and your friends probably admire you for it. The downside of motivation by expectancy, however, is that many of our fondest dreams for tomorrow never materialize. That reality can leave us embittered or, just as often, ceaselessly chasing pots of gold at the end of rainbows, invisible to ourselves. If your score is high in this column, you might want to reflect on the value of tempering expectation-based motivation with other, more immediate goals and rewards.

What should all of this mean to you and your career? In a nutshell, it means you should be performing at a level that will reflect favorably upon your boss. If your boss does not get promoted how can you expect to one-day get promoted into their job? Perhaps coming to an understanding of what motivates you to excel will be beneficial as you prepare for the next job you seek. As you prepare for your next promotion you will need to consider what is required of you in that position.

CHAPTER 4

Understanding What Is Required

In a new job or even in your current situation, it can often be difficult to know for sure what is required of you by the organization. More often than not, the human resources department will have an orientation to help individuals become acclimated to the culture of the organization. However, the very best way to find out anything is to ask questions.

In order to find out what is expected on the job, ask questions of your coworkers about your boss. Coworkers can tell you how the boss wants you to respond to his or her job requirements. This all depends upon which type of organization you are associated with. When asking questions of your manager, make sure you are illuminating their requirements of you, and the questions are designed to help you understand what they are expecting from you.

Not many businesses define specifically what management expects of their employees.[1] The company may provide you with the outcome—like "get the work done by five." But what is the work that must be done by five? If possible, you should ask for a specific set of expectations for both production and culture. Sara Nichols, vice president of finance for Kforce, provides 10 ways you can meet and exceed your boss's expectations and standout as an exceptional employee.[2] Those 10 items are stated next.

Manage Expectations

While it is important to focus on ways to meet and exceed your boss's expectations, first and foremost, your boss will likely want you to manage his or her expectations efficiently. Take the time to understand what the boss expects when it comes to project deadlines and deliverables. By frequently communicating with the boss about his or her expectations around the nature and timing of deliverables, the likelihood of exceeding those expectations can dramatically increase.

Communicate

Whether it is verbal or written, expressing ideas, deadlines, and other messages to your boss efficiently is a must. Effective communication skills can differentiate you as a professional and help your boss gain confidence in your ability to take on new roles and responsibilities. When communicating with the boss, both online and in-person, it is important to craft well-thought-out, concise messages. When crafting your communication, think about the perception you are trying to create and choose your tone and words accordingly.

Ask Questions

In addition to effective communication, it is also important to know when to ask questions. Nichols suggests asking the boss, and even another team member, about additional details regarding project requirements or possible strategies to implement on a new assignment. After you have asked the question, it is vital to listen to the answer. If you ask a question and do not know the answer, be sure to ask clarifying questions until you understand. You cannot come up with a thoughtful solution for a situation if you do not understand the problem. "If your boss notices that you are asking thoughtful questions, they are likely to see you as a crucial contributor to the team who can add value," says Nichols. Just remember to listen to the feedback provided.

Display a Positive Attitude

It is expected that some days at work can be challenging or stressful, when meeting deadlines or working on a budget. However, Nichols says a positive attitude is a must-have when it comes to building a successful team, and it is important to stay optimistic and encouraging in even the most difficult of circumstances. From the moment you meet someone, take notice of their approach. A positive attitude is a key quality that can demonstrate strength of character and can win the respect of your coworkers by making you someone with whom it is easy to do business.

Be a Team Player

Just as it is important to display a positive attitude, most employers appreciate those professionals who are good listeners that work well with others and contribute to the team effort.

All employees should be working toward the same goal, whether that means generating revenue or promoting a positive image of the company. Those employees who align their own goals to the team's goals are likely to be noticed by management.

Become Self-motivated

With little direction, self-motivated employees are the go-getters that take the lead on assignments or research details before important meetings. Be the kind of self-starter that can help your boss save time and allow them to focus on other areas. Employees who routinely rise to new challenges, and demonstrate a high degree of self-motivation, tend to get recognized when the opportunity for advancement is presented.

Keep Your Skills Up-to-Date

As technology evolves, so must professionals. Whether it is the latest version of the software or regulatory changes, Nichols says most bosses will expect their employees to keep their professional skills up-to-date. Staying abreast of the latest developments in your industry can show continuous improvement and help you become a more efficient and effective employee.

Be Flexible

In addition to changes in technology, changes to the organization, goals, and project requirements are inevitable. While it may be a challenge for some, remaining flexible and adapting to these changes can be a crucial skill. Most importantly, she reminds employees to continue to maintain flexibility when changes occur in the workplace.

Pay Attention to Detail

When it comes to overseeing multiple projects, not all bosses may have the time to manage all the specifics. Employees who can pay attention to details and raise concerns may not only have the opportunity to earn the trust of their boss but be recognized for their efforts in spotting errors and correcting any inaccuracies.

Differentiate Yourself

Last but not least, identify what differentiates you professionally from the rest and make it a characteristic that your boss can depend on. Making small efforts such as routinely showing up to work early each day or consistently finding new, more efficient ways to accomplish everyday tasks can help you position yourself as a valuable resource to your boss and team. Nichols says that while many professionals may have the qualifications to do the job, differentiating yourself and what unique elements you can bring to the table will set you apart.

Implement the 10 aforementioned strategies, and you too can stand out as a star employee, an exemplary follower. It is your job to demonstrate to your boss that you can continue to add value to the team and its goals.[3] Ask yourself each day how can I make my boss's job easier? Then you can begin to meet and exceed his or her expectations.

Another item that is needed to be able to meet or exceed the boss's expectations is courage. It is important for you to be courageous as an exemplary follower. Ultimately, there are no formulas for courage; we develop it through determination and practice, self-forgiveness when we fail, and growth when we learn.[4] The act of courage implies that there is a risk involved. There is no need for courage in the absence of risk. An exemplary follower must balance the asking of questions without fear and the needs of providing security for one's family.[5] It may be prudent to develop contingency plans if the need arises.

If you are consistent at performing the day to day tasks of your job and are able to demonstrate the flexibility required to develop contingency plans, you are demonstrating one facet of being trustworthy. It is important for you as a follower to be reliable. There are several things you can do to show you are reliable.

- *Meet your deadlines and fulfill your responsibilities.*[6] You cannot expect your relationship to develop positively if you are not performing up to expectations. If you are having trouble keeping up with your workload, talk with your manager as soon as possible so you can work together to find a solution.
- *Know which of your tasks and responsibilities your manager sees as most critical for meeting your group's goals.*[7] If you are not sure which of your responsibilities takes top priority, you may not be working as efficiently as possible. Schedule time with the manager if you are uncertain about his expectations; don't assume you are on track because you have not heard otherwise.
- *Don't wait for your manager to tell you what to do.*[8] Make his job easier and impress him by taking the initiative to do the things you are sure you need to do without being asked. You may also want to ask for long-term projects that you can work on when you have a lull in your regular assignments.
- *On a personal level, show friendliness and respect toward your manager.*[9] You do not have to be friends with your manager, but it can be easier to establish a comfortable working relationship when you add a more personal dimension. If your manager is receptive, occasionally ask about her family, hobbies, or what movies she has seen lately. Share some information about yourself, too.
- *Focus on solutions, not problems.*[10] Problems inevitably come up. By focusing on possible solutions rather than what went wrong, you will be presenting your manager with a proactive, positive approach that will likely be appreciated.
- *Be a team player.*[11] Helps to keep up your department's morale by being a positive, productive team player. Remember that

your manager has other employees to manage and other responsibilities of which you may not be aware. You can help make his job easier by trying to get along well with everyone on your team, offering support when needed, and being flexible about changes in work routines and assignments.

- *Help your manager succeed.*[12] Making your manager look good is one of the best things you can do to improve or strengthen your relationship. Keep in mind that your manager's success is also good for your career. Look for ways that your skills can complement hers, so that you can help your manager succeed. For example, your manager may be a terrific public speaker, but not so great at using PowerPoint. If that is your strong suit, let your manager know that you are available to help with that. Similarly, be available to help your manager out in a pinch; managers appreciate people who can come to the rescue in a tight situation. Bosses also value those employees who demonstrate loyalty to them and the organization.

Loyalty is an important trait in an employee. A boss who recognizes your support can be a champion for your career and an excellent professional advocate for you. Being loyal to your boss does not mean covering for mistakes or being deceptive in any way. It means supporting your employer's goals and objectives through your own work contributions. Loyalty also means the following topics.

Don't Gossip[13]

The boss is often the topic of gossip in a workplace environment. Don't participate in spreading rumors that speculate about your boss's motives or otherwise engage in talking behind the boss's back. Any time you participate in this kind of talk, your boss will hear of it and question your honesty, reliability, and professionalism. If you hear colleagues talking poorly about your boss, discourage the conversation, say something positive, or leave the conversation, so you are not associated with the behavior.

Back Up Your Boss[14]

Support your boss's ideas among the employees. Offer positive comments in staff meetings and strive to support initiatives, either in word or action. Learn what your boss's strategic objectives are and look for ways you can contribute to their success. If you can advance your boss's agenda through your own work efforts, look for ways to do so. It creates a successful situation for both of you.

Do Your Job Well[15]

You are a reflection of your boss to upper management, and doing your job efficiently and professionally makes your boss look like a competent manager. Don't miss deadlines or do sloppy work, especially if you are working on a task or project that will be a direct reflection of your boss or your staff. For example, if you are putting together financial data for a board meeting presentation, failure to complete your tasks on time will make your boss look out of control of the area.

Make the Boss Look Good[16]

Make your boss look good to others; such as, customers, clients, and the boss's superiors. Acknowledge your manager's contributions and give credit for ideas and concepts. If your boss takes time to mentor you and help you with your career advancement, say, "Thank you." Express your loyalty through honest communication. If you decide to make a career move that takes you outside the company, be forthright about your decision so you can part on good terms.

The final item that is required in fulfilling obligations to the job and the organization is to be truthful.[17] Honesty is vital to making practical changes and identifying who you are and what you want. When you lie about who you are or what you believe, you reinforce the idea that you need to pretend to be someone else or that you are not fundamentally "good enough." Worse, you undermine virtually every other key principle for self-improvement because they are based on the premise that you have identified your authentic self and your goals. This is impossible to achieve if you are denying or deceiving yourself. Without the truth of who you are and what you want, you cannot have clarity in life, and you cannot achieve your dreams because you have no actual direction. Now that you understand what is required of you in order to become an exemplary follower what is next? You need to understand how to communicate effectively.

CHAPTER 5

Communications

I know that you believe you understand what I said, but, I am not sure you realize that what you heard is not what I meant.[1] This statement sums it all; communication is and can be a problem for nearly everyone and at every level in all organizations. In many positions, you may find yourself writing or preparing items for the boss. You may produce work for the boss to sign and move forward. As an exemplary follower, you need to do your absolute best to master this skill, as communication may very well be the key to all of the other skills necessary to succeed.

First, think about why we communicate. The answer to this seemingly complex question is very simple. Human communication has no other purpose than to cause some action of some type: to direct, to inform, to challenge, and to persuade; for example:

- Stand over there.
- I just sent you a text.
- Where's my cell phone?
- This is a great car, you should buy it.[2]

If communication is going to take place there must be six components present: a sender, a message, a channel, a receiver, feedback, and the environment.[3] The sender is the source, the person sending the message. The message is the heart of the discussion and should be clear. The channel or the medium is how the information is transmitted to the receiver. The receiver is the other person to whom the sender is directing the message in whatever form it takes. Communication cannot take place unless there is a sender and a receiver.

Caring

Regardless of the process of communication and how the message is transmitted, the message must display a caring attitude about the circumstances of the message. You must demonstrate that the information is valuable to both yourself and to the receiver. This can be accomplished in many ways. First, in the case of face-to-face communication, your body language and facial expressions can demonstrate your position, whether it is attentive or indifferent. Caring communication is friendly, open, and honest. There are no hidden insults or passive-aggressive tones. Keep your reader's viewpoint in mind, and be empathetic to their needs. Here is an example of an uncaring e-mail:[4]

Jeff,

I wanted to let you know that I do not appreciate how your team always monopolizes the discussion at our weekly meetings. I have many projects, and I really need time to get my team's progress discussed as well. So far, thanks to your department, I haven't been able to do that. Can you make sure they make time for me and my team next week?

Thanks,

Phil

Well, that is hardly courteous! Messages like this can potentially start office-wide fights. So this e-mail does nothing but create bad feelings, and lower productivity and morale. A little bit of caring can go a long way.

Here is a more caring approach:

Hi Jeff,

I wanted to write you a quick note to ask a favor. During our weekly meetings, your team does an excellent job of highlighting their progress. But this uses some of the time available for my team to highlight theirs. I'd really appreciate it if you could give my team a little extra time each week to fully cover their progress reports.

Thanks so much, and please let me know if there's anything I can do for you!

Best,

Phil

Concise

When you are concise in communication, stick to the point and keep it brief. Your audience does not want to read six sentences when three sentences would do just fine.[5]

- Are there any adjectives or *filler words* that you can delete? You can often eliminate words like "for instance," "you see," "definitely," "kind of," "literally," "basically," or "I mean."
- Are there any unnecessary sentences?
- Have you repeated the point many times, in different ways?

Bad Example

Hi Matt,

I wanted to touch base with you about the e-mail marketing campaign we kind of sketched out last Thursday. I really think that our target market is definitely going to want to see the company's philanthropic efforts. I think that could make a big impact, and it would stay in their minds longer than a sales pitch.

For instance, if we talk about the company's efforts to become sustainable, as well as the charity work we're doing in local schools, then the people that we want to attract are going to remember our message longer. The impact will just be greater.

What do you think?

Jessica

This e-mail is too long! There's repetition, and there's plenty of *filler* taking up space.

Good Example

Watch what happens when we're concise and take out the filler words:

Hi Matt,

I wanted to quickly discuss the e-mail marketing campaign that we analyzed last Thursday. Our target market will want to know about the company's philanthropic efforts, especially our goals to become sustainable and help local schools.

This would make a far greater impact, and it would stay in their minds longer than a traditional sales pitch.

What do you think?

Jessica

Straightforward[6]

A straightforward person chooses words carefully in their communication. Words used while talking to a child is different from the words used while talking to an adult. Similarly, usage and choice of words also depends on the gender, geography, education level, and personality. Straightforward people think before they speak, pick words so that the information is exchanged without hurting the other party.

Listening, politeness, and a positive attitude are all traits of straight forwardness. Many think that having good communication skills is speaking well with right words, but you should also remember that listening is yet another element of communication that sometimes speaks more than words. A straightforward customer service executive will listen to all issues from the customer without interrupting. A straightforward person would replace negative words with positive words. All it takes is a little planning and organization of thoughts before uttering the words. Use of positive or neutral words without altering the essence of the message is trait of good conversationalists. Straightforwardness means being polite too. The sound of the language makes a big difference while speaking. A list of interesting tones of the language would include, polite, friendly, kind, courteous, considerate, civil, well-mannered, gracious, and chivalrous.

Truthful

The advantage of telling the truth is that you do not have to remember what you said.

—Mark Twain

Your communications should be truthful, based upon what you know the truth to be. This means that your communications should not be designed to deceive or mislead those with whom you are communicating for or with. As Mark Twain has said, it is far easier to tell the truth, as you do not have to remember what lies you told to which people. As you can see effective communication is very important. The next step is to be able to take the initiative to get things done.

CHAPTER 6

The Three "I"s of Initiative

What does it mean to show initiative at work? It means simply to make your boss's job easy. How does one make the boss's job easier by using initiative? Let us briefly discuss several different assets you can display as an exemplary follower to make your boss's job easy. You should be imaginative, inspirational, and independent.

Imagination

Imagination is the act or power of forming a mental image of something not present to the senses or never before wholly perceived in reality.[1] Albert Einstein once said, "Imagination is everything. It is the preview of life's coming attractions." Your imagination can be one of your greatest personal assets. It allows you to see the world or your new job as full of possibility. When used purposefully, your imagination becomes the trigger of your creative abilities, and you can begin to make your boss's job easier.[2]

1. *Write it down.* What have you imagined? What does this fantasy look like, and how does it influence your existence? Describe it in detail. As you write, allow the details to add clarity to your vision. If some important aspect is unclear, read your description and then close your eyes and concentrate on what you see.

2. *Tell me your fantasies, and I will show you your dreams. Write them down, and I will read you your future.* The goal here is to put your mental image, and the feelings connected with it, into words that accurately describe your idea. The written word will introduce your fantasy to the physical world. It will now live in black and white on a sheet of paper that you can carry around and read whenever and wherever you want.

3. *Define the sequence.* Every vision has a logical sequence to its understanding. Let's use a home in the country as an example. First, you need to decide if it is a home you want to build, or one that already exists. If you are going to build it (or have it built), then the sequence would involve a piece of property, a house plan, permits, site preparation. Each sequential step will require a certain amount of time, money, or both.

4. If you want to buy an existing home, then you need to figure out where to begin your search. Does it need to be near a city that will support your work? Does it need to have room for raising horses or some other important purpose? How much money do you need for a down payment? Answering these questions will allow you to see what comes first in the understanding sequence.

5. *Create a plan of action.* Once you have defined the sequence, make a plan. What can you do right now to start actively moving toward the realization of your vision? What will you do next? Figure out how to start unfolding this new reality. You will probably discover extra steps along the way, but don't worry about that now. Figure out a tentative plan and write it down. The most important thing is to get the ball moving in the right direction without getting bogged down in too many details.

6. *Start taking action.* Action is now an essential component for the realization. Find something to do and start doing it. If you want that cute little house in the country, start looking. If you need more money to make it happen, figure out how to start making more money. Don't let the lack of money prevent you from continuing your search. Looking is free, and it keeps the vision alive. It also keeps your mind motivated to find a solution to the money aspect. If you are going to build a house, start drawing up floor plans and figure out what style you want. Do this while you continue to look for property. Keep taking action, so your mind stays focused on your vision. *With action comes clarity, purpose, and direction.*

7. *Keep track of your progress.* One of the things that can help us stay motivated during this process is to recognize our progress continually. Every single time you accomplish even the tiniest goal, write it down, check it off, and celebrate your progress. Give yourself credit

for bringing your vision that much closer to understanding. Make sure you always take time to acknowledge your accomplishments along the way. To continue the realization process just keep your vision alive in your imagination, keep adding clarity to it, and keep taking action in the right direction.

Inspiration

We all know people who are encouraging. However, just how does one inspire others? Here are 10 simple ways you can inspire people to be their best:[3]

1. *Be a good example.* People watch what you do more than they listen to what you say. Be someone worth emulating.
2. *Care about others.* People do not care about how much you know until they know how much you care. Ask questions. Take a genuine interest in people.
3. *Encouragement.* Everyone goes through tough times. When you support people and encourage them through these times, you'll be encouraging them to see the best in themselves and the situation.
4. *Be inspired yourself.* Look for people, ideas, environments, and knowledge that you find inspiring and motivating.
5. *Share from your own experience.* You have more to share than you realize. Mine the rich experiences of your life and share your wisdom from your unique point of view. You may be the only one who can touch someone with your inspiring message.
6. *Be vulnerable.* Be willing to share your failures, as well as your successes. Others will relate to you. They'll understand that they are not the only ones with challenges.
7. *Tell stories.* Facts tell, and stories sell. They inspire, too. We learn best from parables, and we all need to develop our own inspiring stories.
8. *Be a good communicator.* Increasing your ability to communicate effectively is a critical element for you to inspire others. Watch how you speak and what you say. Invest in your communication skills.
9. *Challenge people.* Many of us have had teachers who at times seemed more like tormentors than mentors. They challenged us to do our

best, and we were better for it. Practice *carefrontation*—the careful and caring confrontation of others.

10. *Read*. It may not follow that all readers are leaders, but certainly all leaders are readers. Stay informed. Share what you read with others. Tell people about books that have inspired you. Share the knowledge.[4]

Independent Thinking

In order for you to come up with truly unique, creative ideas, you must become an independent thinker. Our brains are full of recycled ideas we've already heard from others, but you can learn to think independently, or come up with novel ideas, with a few easy psychological tips and tools.[5] Consequently, your natural tendency is to draw on your experience to come up with solutions to problems. Independent thinking requires you to break that mold. Try these three strategies to prompt your brain to think more independently:[6]

Place a Lot of Constraints on the Problem[7]

Paradoxically, open-ended problems are the enemy of independent thinking. Instead, give yourself limitations. Rule out elements of the solution that look expected or natural. For example, can you make a bank that has no tellers? Can you write a book that has no beginning? The constraints should force you to consider an unfamiliar scenario, and you should try as many of them as you work toward a viable solution.

Combine Ideas That Seem Ill-Matched[8]

When you are trying to solve a problem, your memory will retrieve solutions or concepts that seem like logical matches, often because others have used that match already. To think differently, consider ideas that don't seem compatible at all. For example, what if you made a dating website that worked as Wikipedia? Alternatively, what if you found a way to open a can using only airplane parts? Many of your ideas will fail, but any that succeed are likely to be unique.

Take the Bird's Eye View[9]

When you are trying to solve a problem, zoom out to see variables that others might overlook. Ask yourself, what is the purpose of solving this problem? What would happen if I succeed? Moreover, how can I find a solution that makes that outcome work? For example, Thomas Edison saw that houses would need to be wired for electricity if people were going to buy light bulbs. To send power over long distances, you need a high-voltage bulb. Edison was the only inventor who realized this, so he was the one who made history. Once you have begun to take the initiative to make things happen you will need to maintain your positive mental attitude.

CHAPTER 7

Positive Attitude

Our beliefs about what we are and what we can be precisely determine what we can be.

—Anthony Robbins

A positive attitude—optimism, expectancy, and enthusiasm—makes everything in business easier. A positive attitude boosts you up when you are down and supercharges you when you are already "on a roll."[1]

A positive attitude sounds like something one should have at all times. However, I have been curious for a long time about how exactly this works. For example, I have been positive many times that I was going to win the lottery, and it has not happened yet. So maybe my attitude was not positive but perhaps just hopeful. Is there a difference between being hopeful and having a positive attitude? The great tragedy is that the world is full of people who are trying to change the outside world without going to work on the one thing that they can control, their own thinking.[2] Therefore, it appears a positive attitude is not something you wish for, but something you have to decide is worth working for, and you have to work to earn that attitude.

Here are some tips from three different experts to help you work toward earning a positive attitude. Can you identify the techniques they have in common?

Jeffrey Keller frames it this way.

Remember That You Control Your Attitude[3]

Attitude does not emerge from what happens to you, but instead from how you choose to interpret what happens to you. In each case, the person is deciding how to understand the event and, therefore, controlling how he or she feels about it (i.e., approach).

Adopt Beliefs That Frame Events in a Positive Way[4]

Your beliefs and rules about life and work determine how you interpret events and, therefore, your attitude. Choose to adopt *strong* beliefs that create a good attitude rather than ideas that create a bad attitude. To use sales as an example:

- *Situation:* The first sales call of the day goes poorly.
  - o *Weak:* A lousy first call means that I'm off my game and today will suck.
  - o *Strong:* Every sales call is different, so the next will probably be better.

- *Situation:* A customer reduces the amount of an order at the last minute!
  - o *Weak:* Customers who change orders can't be trusted.
  - o *Strong:* Customers who change orders are more likely to be satisfied!

- *Situation:* A big sales win comes seemingly out of nowhere.
  - o *Weak:* Even a blind pig finds an acorn once in a while.
  - o *Strong:* You never know when something wonderful will happen!

Create a "Library" of Positive Thoughts[5]

Spend at least 15 minutes every morning to read, view, or listen to something inspirational or motivational. If you do this regularly, you'll have those thoughts and feelings ready at hand (or rather, ready in your mind), when events don't go exactly the way you'd prefer.

Ignore Whiners and Complainers[6]

Whiners and complainers see the world through crap-colored glasses. They'd rather talk about what's irreparably wrong, rather than make things better. More importantly, complainers can't bear to see somebody else happy and satisfied. If you tell a complainer about a success that you've experienced, they'll congratulate you, but their words ring hollow. You can sense they'd rather you told them about what's making you miserable.

Use a More Positive Vocabulary[7]

The words that come out of your mouth aren't just a reflection of what's in your brain—they're programming your brain how to think. Therefore, if you want to have a positive attitude, your vocabulary must be consistently positive. Therefore,

- Stop using negative phrases such as "I can't," "It's impossible," or "This won't work." These statements program you for negative results;
- Whenever anyone asks "How are you?" rather than "Hangin' in there," or "Okay, I guess..." respond with "Terrific!" or "Never felt better!" And mean it;

- When you're feeling angry or upset substitute neutral words for emotionally loaded ones. Rather than saying "I'm enraged!" say, "I'm a bit annoyed. . . ."

An additional set of tips for learning how to establish a positive attitude comes from Declan O'Flaherty:[8]

Remember That You Are Powerful[9]

Most of the time we have no idea what we are supposed to be doing, or who we are supposed to be imitating; most of the time we conform to the external environment. We play roles and cover up our true selves by identifying with "things" that end up defining who we think we are. Your job or position should not define you as an individual.

Choose to Embrace Life[10]

Let go and embrace the moment, whether it contains an obstacle or an opportunity. Stop fussing over trivial matters and start focusing on what's important to you. Don't go through life expecting things to change. Life becomes hard and unfair when we decide to complain about things rather than trying to change them ourselves. Wake up to the truth that life is not a practice-run. Be bold and courageous, and make decisions that benefit your growth. Put yourself on your imaginary death-bed and realize that time stands still for no one. Start as soon as possible to make any necessary changes you may need to. Take the first step before more time gradually passes by while you stand still stagnating.

Realize That You Get to Control Your Reactions[11]

We create our outside reality by the thoughts and beliefs we maintain about life in general. What we believe in our inner world, we see in our outer world—not the other way around. We all have problems, and we are often tested by circumstances outside of our control. Even though you may not be in control of what's going on outside of you, you can control your reaction to those situations. You have more control than you think.

Know That No One Is Better Qualified[12]

We place far too much emphasis on other people's opinions about us, often to the exclusion of our own. This takes us away from our own personal power. No matter what anybody says about you, it doesn't hold any significance to who you truly are unless you identify or agree with them. Stop identifying with other people's opinions and become aware of how you see yourself. Nobody knows you better than you do. Never accept another person's reality as your own. Always believe that you can achieve anything you put your mind to. And, most importantly, never let another person's opinion of you affect what you think about yourself.

Love Yourself[13]

You have arrived. Everything you need is right here. Cut out the distractions, open your eyes, and see that you already have everything in your possession to be happy, loved, and fulfilled. Be yourself and completely accept everything that you are.

Stay Cool[14]

If someone cuts you off in traffic or skips the queue at the movie, you may feel the need to respond in a negative manner. We allow what other people do to dictate our behavior. You are responsible for your own action, regardless of how rude other people may act. If it is hard to stay calm, remember: you are the one who loses in the end, if you lose the lesson. Remember that your responsibilities equal your ability to control your response.[15]

Melanie Thomassian provides an additional point of view about establishing a positive mental attitude (PMA) in this method.

Focus on the Present[16]

How often do you find that things you worry about for days end up not happening at all, or not being as big a problem as you thought? But, by focusing on the present as much as possible, you can minimize the worries and fears that lead to negative emotions.

Use Positive Language[17]

Do you ever notice how much of what you say is negative? Some people constantly complain about the weather, their work, their spouse, their neighbors, and any number of other things. However, it's good to remind ourselves that our words are shaped by our thoughts, and the more we can look for positive things to say, the more positive our thoughts will become. Make it your endeavor to commit to positive thinking. So, each day when you wake up give yourself a mini pep talk: What do you want to achieve? How will you react to trying different conditions? How will you avoid negative thoughts? Remember, thinking positive is a habit, which means it's possible to learn how to do it.

Accept When Things Aren't Perfect[18]

It can be difficult to let go of the need for perfection and control in your life, but sometimes it's very liberating to simply accept that things will not always go the way you hoped, and that's okay. Sometimes things happen that are out of your control, and rather than wasting your energy on negative emotions, it's better to just admit that things didn't go the way you planned or wanted.

Mix With Positive People[19]

It's a fact of human nature that we tend to mimic the people with whom we spend the most time. Think of how teenagers tend to conform to the social code of their friends. It's the same for everyone else, too. So, the more frequently you spend time with positive thinking people, the more likely it is that you will begin to think and act in a similar fashion. Also, don't underestimate the power of laughing either, it has an excellent way of reducing stress, connecting you with those around you, and making you feel better all around.

Contribute in a Meaningful Way[20]

One of the best ways to feel more confident is to contribute to your community in some way. It can be tremendously uplifting to help others, whether it's through the use of your time, skills, or financial contributions. As well as the good feelings that come with making a difference in someone's life, contributing your time and effort to a cause, allows you a brief escape from your current problems, and perhaps may even allow you to see your troubles in a different light.

Keep Learning[21]

Develop a curiosity about the world around you, and the people in it. No matter what situation you are in right now, there is always something we can learn from it. Taking a real interest in life gives you energy, it helps create new ideas in your mind, and gives you a different way of thinking about things, which can have a positive impact on your life as a whole.

Be Grateful[22]

Spend a little time each day thinking of things that you are truly grateful for in your life. Reminding yourself of all the reasons you have to be grateful, helps to maintain some focus on your situation. Being thankful will often turn initial anger or frustration into something more positive. Remember, we all have weaknesses, but focusing on your strengths prevents them getting the better of us. A good practice to get into is that of keeping a gratitude journal. This is where you make a note of at least five things that make you happy or thankful each day. This is one of the best ways to foster the habit of gratitude. Finally, keep in mind that how you view your life is *your choice*. No one is forcing you to have a negative attitude, so take control and change it for a happier, more energetic, and more enthusiastic life.

There are some common myths or misconceptions about maintaining a positive attitude. These are that (1) negative thinking is more realistic, (2) people with a PMA expect anything can happen if they wish for it, (3) positive thinking does not change reality, (4) positive thinkers have no insight into the real world, and (5) people with a PMA are annoying and cheesy.[23]

Negative Thinking Is More Realistic[24]

Have you ever heard a negative person say that they aren't negative; they just are realistic? This myth keeps people locked in a negative reality of their own creation. A person's thoughts, whether positive or negative, do have an effect on their environment. If you think negatively, your mind will automatically seek out confirmation that the world is a terrible place. Seeing is believing, and your mind reinforces your belief that reality is negative. See how it's a downward spiral of negativity? If you expect negative results, you are less likely to take risks and try new things. Negative thinking masks your impressions in fear. Positive thinking works the same way. With a PMA, you'll seek out positive choices and expect positive results. This helps you move past fear and try things that others may think "can't be done."

A person's thinking helps determine their reality. Negative thinking is practical for the negative thinker, but only because their ideas make it true. Ironically, the positive thinker also sees reality, just in a different light. Both types of people see their own reality, and both consider it *the* reality.

People With a PMA Expect Anything Can Happen If They Wish for It[25]

Those who don't believe in positive thinking imagine that positive thinkers expect that their desire will manifest itself if they simply think positively about it. This couldn't be further from the truth. Everyone who accomplishes anything—whether it's earning a million dollars or becoming an award-winning actor—accomplish it the same way; by taking action. Positive people have an edge because they believe the object of their desire is attainable. They come from a can-do mindset. Their actions are not based on fear or scarcity, but based on possibilities. Thus, a positive attitude helps a person manifest their desires, not only by dreaming about it, but by inspiring the person to take action.

It's the action behind the attraction that makes the dream come true.

Positive Thinking Doesn't Change Reality[26]

People who believe this myth see a problem and believe that positive thinking will only ignore the ugliness of their reality. The truth is positive thinking doesn't ignore the problem; it helps you see the problem in a new light. In fact, you don't even see "problems" as problems. Think about it;

regardless of how you react to an external condition, the situation will still be the same. If being upset doesn't change the outcome of a past situation, would not it serve you, and your health, to see the positives?

A PMA creates a mindset of abundance, enthusiasm, and solutions. Instead of thinking about what cannot be done, a positive thinker will not be constrained by cannot. A positive thinker is free to think of new ways to solve problems because they are not limited by a fear of failure. When we are in a state of abundance, we provide a fertile ground for opportunities and make dreams a reality. We are in a state of allowance, openly accepting the gifts of life to flow to us. When I realized this principle and shifted my thinking habits, miracles started popping up in my life. A PMA can—and indeed does—change reality by allowing a person to act in an entirely different way, thus harvesting entirely different results.

Successful men become successful only because they acquire the habit of thinking in terms of success.

—Napoleon Hill

Positive Thinkers Have No Clue About The Real World[27]

It's easy to believe that people with a PMA have perfect lives and have never dealt with real world hardships. Maybe people wouldn't be so positive if they'd endured a few difficult times in their lives. But the truth is that this is really just a justification for negative thinking. It would be difficult to find a positive person who hasn't had real and serious trials in their lives. They have faced disappointment, death of loved ones, physical handicap, and pretty much the range of human experiences with which we all deal. The difference is that these people do not allow those events change their outlook. A PMA means that you are in control of your own thoughts and feelings. Every person has sorrows and trials that test them to the core, but only some people have the courage to act positively and with grace. A PMA doesn't mean a person has sidestepped a hard life. It simply means that they want to see and take part in the good things life has to offer, as opposed to only the negative.

We cannot avoid suffering but we can choose how to cope with it, find
meaning in it, and move forward with renewed purpose.
—Viktor E. Frankl

People With a PMA Are Annoying and Cheesy[28]

Okay, let's admit it, some types of positive people **are** a little cheesy and, sometimes, can be very obnoxious. I am describing the people who spout platitudes and expect everything to be perfect no matter what. You know the people I am describing. But truly positive people are not Tony Robbins infomercials. Positive people have real thoughts and have setbacks and discouragement just like everyone else, but they are also resilient and look for ways to stay positive. Truly positive people do not expect perfection, but, rather, they expect that every event is the best thing that could have happened at that moment. It is the only event that happened at that moment. Now that you're considering the event, that moment has past. You cannot go back and change the moment, so you have to accept what happened was the best, and move on to the next moment. Even in external circumstances that seem out of our control, we can always control our internal response. In fact, it's the only thing over which we have absolute control. This PMA can lead to great things, and where much is given much is expected. This leads to taking responsibility for those things in your control.

CHAPTER 8

Responsibility

Have you ever been in a situation where you had the responsibility to accomplish a task but did not have the authority that goes along with the responsibility? Most of us can answer that question in the affirmative. Having responsibility is the duty or obligation to act.[1] Taking responsibility is acknowledging and accepting the choices you have made, the actions you have taken, and the results they have led to. True autonomy leads to both having responsibility and taking responsibility. Taking responsibility is fulfilling your role in life. Responsibility is an essential element of integrity; it is the congruence of what you think, what you say, and what you do. Responsibility is essential for reciprocity, trust, and for maintaining honesty.[2]

Definitions[3]

1. Having a duty or obligation to act.
2. Acknowledging and accepting the choices you have made, the actions you have taken, and the results they have led to.
3. Able to meet commitments made to yourself and others
4. Keeping the promises you make.
5. Doing everything you say you will do, or have led others to expect from you. Do what you say.

Honesty

Honesty is vital to making effective changes and identifying who you are and what you want. Being honest is critical at every level of your life, not just with yourself. When you are dishonest, you are effectively saying that the only way to get things out of life is to lie or cheat. In this modern world of marketing spin and half truths, maintaining honesty might be seen as a bit of a challenge. But in reality it is not difficult, we always know at a fundamental level what is right. Being honest does require a high level of self-discipline and is often difficult to do at first because we have all gotten so used to those little lies and pretenses that seemed to make life simpler. The good news is that with practice being honest gets a lot easier, especially when you realize that others start to identify your authenticity, and their respect grows accordingly.[4]

Integrity

Integrity is not a theory or philosophy it is concrete and real; it is efficient and effective. Acting with integrity is doing things right especially when no one is looking.[5] There are four components to integrity: personal convictions (what we believe), stated values (what we say we believe), operational values (what we actually do), and ethical principles (what we should do).[6] Integrity is a quality of character demonstrated by the moral commitment and courage necessary to maintain consistency between what we believe, what we say, what we do, and what we are morally obliged to do. In other words, are your actions different from what you say? Do you say one thing and then do another? John Wooden said, "If you don't have the time to do it right, when will you have the time to do it over." You have the time to do the right thing and you can choose that path.

Take a moment to think about your personal convictions (remember these are what we believe). Now that you have your personal convictions in mind, think if they are the same as your stated values (what you say you believe). Go beyond these stated values and try to determine if you follow through and put your stated values into action; this is your operational values. This should bring you to your ethical principles, which is what we should do.

Personal Responsibility

If you could kick the person in the pants responsible for most of your trouble, you wouldn't sit for a month.

—Theodore Roosevelt

What is personal responsibility? It is taking conscious control of your responses to the events and circumstances in your life. You *are* responsible for yourself, whether you like it or not. What you do with your life and what you have done already is up to you. While you may not be able to control everything that happens to you, you are nevertheless responsible for how you think, act, and feel in response to those things.[7] Personal responsibility is the willingness to both accept the importance of standards that society establishes for individual behavior and to make strenuous personal efforts to live by those standards.[8] But personal responsibility also means that when individuals fail to meet expected standards, they do not look around for some factor outside themselves to blame. The demise of personal responsibility occurs when individuals blame their family, their peers, their economic circumstances, or their society for their failure to meet standards.[9] There may be no more impactful thing you can do for yourself than to take responsibility for your life. There are benefits of accepting personal responsibility.[10]

Some of the benefits of accepting personal responsibility are freedom, respect, and trust from those around you, and fewer negative emotions. Freedom can manifest itself by allowing for personal development in general. By acknowledging your role in the process, you give yourself the opportunity to improve. When you accept personal responsibility, you gain the freedom to create your life, anyway you want it.[11] Let's say you make a mistake while working on a project at work. If you admit your mistake, people are more likely to believe you about other things you do. Your word has more meaning to other people when you take responsibility. But it's not just a matter of trust. You also earn lots of respect when you take responsibility for your actions.[12] There are all sorts of negative emotions that come with not accepting personal responsibility. When you blame others, you may feel anger or resentment toward that person. You will almost invariably feel guilty or ashamed. I call this the "nose picker syndrome." If you catch me doing something I know I should not be doing, like picking my nose, the first thing I do is get mad at you (I blame you) then I feel guilty and angry with myself because you caught me doing something I know I should not do.

What does all this have to do with being a better follower and in turn becoming a better leader? If you take responsibility for your actions, you will become more of an asset to your boss. The boss will come to realize that you are someone upon whom he can count on. You need to make a conscious decision to become that person responsible for the decisions and actions you take. But you cannot just say you have decided to take personal responsibility, you have to make true by taking action. Accept responsibility for who you are right now. It's not other people who made you the way you are, but only your thoughts and actions. Sure, many of those thoughts and actions were conditioned into you by your family, society, friends, or other external influences. But it is you alone who had the thought or performed the action. And it is you alone who must take responsibility for them. You do not need to be happy with your situation or your life as it is; you just need to accept yourself and the fact that you are the one who got yourself there. While negative circumstances may have had a significant impact on you, and you may have experienced huge amounts of social conditioning, dwelling on them or blaming others won't help you improve your situation. Only through accepting personal responsibility can you move forward.[13]

Here are some actions that help in the process: recognize your choices, take the blame, and accept yourself and your circumstances.[14] Recognize that you always have choices, and you should accept responsibility for the person you are. It is not other people who made you the way you are, but only your thoughts and actions. Many external forces condition our thoughts; these forces can come from our family, friends, or society as a whole. But you are the person making the choice, and you must take responsibility for the action. Remember, the choices and decisions you have made have allowed you to be found in the circumstances you find yourself in today. Dwelling on your choices or blaming others will not improve your situation; only through accepting personal responsibility can you move forward.[15]

Suppose you make a mistake while working on a special project for the boss. If you admit that mistake to your boss, you will garner respect from the boss and your coworkers.[16] Your word now has more meaning as the result of taking personal responsibility for your actions. But it not just a matter of trust, you also earn respect in this manner when you take personal responsibility for your actions.

There are many negative emotions that come with not accepting personal responsibility. When you blame others, you may feel anger or resentment toward that person. You will almost invariably feel guilty or ashamed. The worst part about denying responsibility is an overall sense of powerlessness. When you feel like you don't have control over your life, you can easily become depressed. You need to make a conscious decision to become the sole person responsible for your life, and you need to make that decision now. But you cannot just say you have decided to take personal responsibility and then have it be true. Surrendering responsibility is a habit that you need to remove, and here is how.

You have to recognize that you have choices.[17] At any given time and in any given situation, you have a choice of how to respond. It does not matter how dire your circumstances are. You could be locked away in an extraordinary rendition prison, but you still control your mental state. You can choose to focus on something positive, no matter how negative a situation you find yourself. Resolve from this point forward you will look at the choices you have available to you instead of feeling constrained.

As a result of having and taking advantage of your choices, do not be afraid to take a risk or make an important decision. Remember you did not ride a bicycle the very first time you got on the thing. When you learned to walk as a young child, you toppled over a few times. So do not be afraid that you are going to crash or mess up. Just keep thinking about what the results might be if you do not take responsibility for your actions. So, when there is a problem, do not ask yourself who is to blame. Instead, ask yourself: "What could I have done differently in order to get the results I want?" When you ask yourself this question it may inevitably lead to you coming up with answers to simple or complex problems, in other words problem solving.

CHAPTER 9

Problem Solving

We all solve problems on a daily basis, in academic situations, at work, and in our day-to-day lives. Any job will bring problems that must be faced. In order for you to make your boss's job easy, it is important to have the right skills to resolve these problems, and the personal **resilience** to handle the challenges and pressure they may cause. To solve problems, you need to be able to[1]

- Evaluate information or situations
- Break them down into their key components
- Consider various ways of approaching and resolving them
- Decide on the most appropriate of these ways

Analytical and critical thinking skills help you to evaluate the problem and to make decisions.[2] A logical and methodical approach is best in some circumstances: for example, you will need to be able to draw on your academic or subject knowledge to identify solutions of practical or technical nature. In other situations, using creativity or lateral thinking will be necessary to come up with ideas for resolving the problem and finding fresh approaches. To make your boss's job easier, you will need skills such as communication, persuasion, and negotiation.

Here are some different ways to solve problems.

Whatever issues you are faced with, some steps are fundamental:[3]

- Identify the problem
- Define the problem
- Examine the options
- Act on a plan
- Look at the consequences

In order to learn to solve problems, there are many different roadmaps and guides to help you, but most of them have the following steps in common:[4]

1. Evaluate the problem by

- Clarifying the nature of a problem
- Formulating questions
- Gathering information systematically
- Collating and organizing data
- Condensing and summarizing information
- Defining the desired objective

2. Manage the problem by

- Using the information gathered effectively;
- Breaking down a problem into smaller, more manageable, parts;
- Using techniques such as brainstorming and lateral thinking to consider options;
- Analyzing these options in greater depth;
- Identifying steps that can be taken to achieve the objective.

3. Decision making

- Deciding between the possible options for what action to take.
- Deciding on further information to be gathered before taking action.
- Deciding on resources (time, funding, staff, etc.) to be allocated to this problem.

4. Resolve the problem by

- Implementing action;
- Providing information to other stakeholders;
- Delegating tasks;
- Reviewing progress.

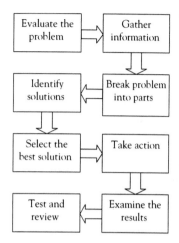

5. Examine the results by

- Monitoring the outcome of the action taken;
- Reviewing the problem and problem-solving process to avoid similar situations in the future.

At any stage of this process, it may be necessary to return to an earlier stage—for example, if additional problems arise or if the solution does not appear to be working as desired.

Here are some other ways to solve problems that may or may not be familiar to you:[5]

- *Algorithm:*[6] An algorithm is a step-by-step procedure that will always produce a correct solution. A mathematical formula is a good example of a problem-solving algorithm. While an algorithm guarantees an accurate answer, it is not always the best approach to problem solving. This strategy is not practical for many situations because it can be so time-consuming. For example, if you were trying to figure out all of the possible number combinations to a lock using an algorithm, it would take a very long time.
- *Heuristics:*[7] A heuristic is a mental rule-of-thumb strategy that may or may not work in certain situations. Unlike algorithms,

heuristics does not always guarantee a correct solution. However, using this problem-solving strategy does allow people to simplify complex problems and reduce the total number of possible solutions to a more manageable set.

- *Trial-and-error:*[8] A trial-and-error approach to problem solving involves trying a number of different solutions and ruling out those that do not work. This approach can be a good option if you have a very limited number of options available. If there are many different choices, you are better off narrowing down the possible options using another problem-solving technique before attempting trial-and-error.

- *Insight:*[9] In some cases, the solution to a problem can appear as a sudden insight. According to researchers, insight can occur because you realize that the problem is similar to something that you have dealt with in the past, but in most cases, the underlying mental processes that lead to insight happen outside of awareness.

There are a number of different obstacles that can interfere with our ability to solve a problem quickly and efficiently. Researchers have described a number of these mental obstacles, which include functional fixedness, irrelevant information, and assumptions.[10] Functional fixedness refers to the tendency to view problems only in their customary manner. Functional fixedness prevents people from fully seeing all of the different options that might be available to find a solution. When you are trying to solve a problem, it is important to distinguish between information that is relevant to the issue and irrelevant data that can lead to faulty solutions. When a problem is very complex, the easier it becomes to focus on misleading or irrelevant information. When dealing with a problem, people often make assumptions about the constraints and barriers that prevent certain solutions.

Another useful analogy for problem solving is to think of the problem as a maze.

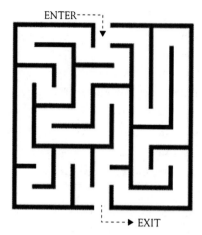

To solve the problem, you need to travel from the starting point, called the initial state, to the endpoint, called the goal state. The initial state includes all of the knowledge and resources you currently have available. The goal state refers to the solution that you want to reach. To get from the initial state to the goal state, you have a number of tools you can use, called operators.

In a maze, these operators might be *left turn* and *right turn*. The set of possible ways to travel from the initial state to the goal state is called the problem space.

Generate and Test

The most obvious way to attempt to solve a problem is simply to mentally test every possible path leading from the initial state to the goal state. This imaginary process of trial and error, called the generate-and-test strategy, considers all possibilities available at every step. However, generate and test is not a realistic problem-solving method for most complex problems as there will be far more potential solutions than time will allow to test. Instead, we must rely on strategies that consider only a subset of the possibilities.

Hill-climbing Strategy

One strategy that can be used is the "hill-climbing strategy." The hill-climbing strategy always moves you toward a solution. Imagine that you want to solve a maze using this strategy. At every fork, you would take the direction that leads toward the exit. However, there are problems with this strategy; the correct path sometimes does not follow this specific direction you think you are headed, and you miss the exit. This is also true of more complex problems, like the river-crossing type. For example:

Three missionaries and three cannibals want to get to the other side of the river. There is a small boat, which can fit only two. To prevent a tragedy, there can never be more cannibals than missionaries together.

One cannibal and one missionary there, missionary back.
Two cannibals there, one cannibal back.
Two missionaries there, one missionary and one cannibal back.
Two missionaries there, one cannibal back.
This one cannibal takes the remaining cannibals to the other side.

Subproblems Strategy

Another, more effective strategy is to break each problem down into a few subproblems. Evidence suggests that people work problems through this way. When working through complex problems, people often tend to work quickly at some points and pause at others. Analysis of their progress suggests that they work quickly when solving a subproblem, and work slowly when deciding what subproblem to tackle next. Smaller problems are easier to solve because there are fewer possible paths to consider.

Working Backwards

Some problems, especially unfamiliar ones, are best-solved by starting at the goal state and working backward toward the initial state. Many people solve mazes in this way, because there are fewer choices to consider in the end than in the beginning. This strategy, while not always helpful, can reduce the overwhelming number of paths available from the initial state.

Reasoning by Analogy

One method that works for many different types of problems is reasoning by analogy. In reasoning by analogy, the problem-solver uses his or her knowledge about previous, similar problems to find out the best way to solve the current one. The use of analogies hinges on familiarity since analogies are not helpful without some previous experience with similar problems. Analogies are simply patterns in the structures of problems. Because experts are more likely to see patterns in the structures of problems, as we saw in the section on expertise, they are best at reasoning by analogy. Novices tend to examine the superficial aspects of the problem, such as comparing two problems that are both about flowers, rather than the structural aspects of how the problem is set up, such as comparing two problems that both require subtraction.

Mental Imagery in Problem Solving

Mental imagery is often useful in problem solving. Verbal descriptions of problems can become confusing, and a mental image can clear away excessive detail to bring out important aspects of the problem. Imagery is most useful with problems that hinge on some spatial relationship. However, if the problem requires an unusual solution, mental imagery alone can be misleading, since it is difficult to change one's understanding of a mental image. In many cases, it helps to draw a concrete picture since a picture can be turned around, played with, and reinterpreted, yielding new solutions in a way that a mental image cannot. There are many models for problem solving and many of them will require teamwork.

CHAPTER 10

Teamwork

Andrew Carnegie said, "Teamwork is the ability to work together toward a common vision; the ability to direct individual accomplishments toward organizational objectives. It is the fuel that allows common people to attain uncommon results." Being on a work team is very similar to being a member of an athletic team, such as, baseball, basketball, soccer, or any other team sport. Much of what you learned as you played on an athletic team can be transferred to a work team. Let us use the game of basketball as an example. In basketball, one person can dribble the ball down the court, shoot, and make a basket. The five individuals who make up the team can play the game in the singular manner. However, each of the five players on the team has a different set of skills and abilities. So the individuals who make up the team, work together to put different individuals into positions in order to take advantage of the skills each possesses. The following eight items can illuminate your path to becoming an effective team player.

Listening[1]

Teamwork means working with others, so putting only your ideas forward and not listening to others is not teamwork. You will need to take the time to listen to other people. Having other individuals' input, and not just your own, is important for making the best decisions, and for the team to respect each other.

Other team-members may be able to spot flaws in your idea, which will mean improvements can be made. You can also discuss their ideas, looking at the pros and cons. Listening is an essential skill that you will have to learn if you want to improve your teamwork skills.

Sharing[2]

While listening to other people's thoughts and ideas is essential, if no one is willing to share their ideas with each other, the team won't get very far. People will have to be willing to share an idea; don't leave it to everybody else, make sure you have some input. It will not only give you more confidence within the team but can also help to encourage others to put forward their ideas. Don't hold back because you want the credit for yourself, and you don't want others to steal the limelight, it's not the end of the world. Just be more laid back about it and care more about helping the team out, not just yourself.

Communication[3]

For a team to work effectively and for team working skills to be made manifest, communication *must* take place, whether we like it or not. Not just communication, but effective communication. It's no good talking about the weather when you need to be dealing with the situation at hand; although, it's good you have the confidence to talk. Teams come up against problems and obstacles, but without effective communication, how will a team overcome these?—it simply can't. So try to communicate.

Don't Let Sore Relationships Affect Your Input[4]

When working with others, it's not uncommon for people to not get along with each other. Maybe something outside of the team has happened between these people, maybe you just don't get along, however, don't let this put a downer on your input team. When you let sore relationships get in the way of making the correct decisions, or you refuse to help the team because of this, you're only hurting the team. Not only that, but people will lose respect for you if you can't be mature enough to put it behind you.

Willingness to Accept[5]

A good team member will be able to have all of the other qualities on this list, as well as having a willingness to accept team decisions and roads of development. It can be very easy to not run with the idea that was chosen over yours, but having the ability to do so will allow the group to make better progress. Believe it or not, it's also good for keeping team morale up, as things run much smoother when all team members are willing to accept and participate in the idea 100 percent. It's no good to have somebody on the team who hinders rather than helps.

Support[6]

A good team that works together shouldn't just be a group of individuals working together, but should in a sense form an individual as a whole, made from all of the individual team members. Different individuals of the team will have different personalities and characteristics, meaning different levels of encouragement and support will be needed. Being able to recognize when somebody needs encouragement or support is a skill that will come over time, but is great for team morale. It also allows you to become closer to that person or people, showing that you care what is happening to them, further tightening the team together.

Patience[7]

As discussed in previous points, working in a team will require you to work with different individuals. Different individuals will have different personalities; some will be loud and boisterous, others will be quiet and timid. As a member of the team, patience will be needed on your behalf. If you were to lose your patience and become angry at other team members, it could affect team relationships and make it awkward for the group as a whole. Patience will be needed for working with everybody; it takes time for a group to find its footing and can take even longer for a team to work and gel together nicely.

Hard Work[8]

It's great if a team can listen to one another, it's great if a team can share ideas with each other, and it's great if a team can communicate effectively, but without hard work—what's the point.

Hard work is where the ideas presented are put into practice and are tackled head-on. Hard work is great for getting a team to gel and great for encouraging other team members to do the same.

William G. Dyer, W. Gibb Dyer Jr., and Jeffrey H. Dyer in their book, *Team Building: Proven Strategies for Improving Team Performance,* identify what they call the four Cs of team development. Those four Cs are context, composition, competencies, and change.[9] The discussion that follows will assist in the development of your team building skills as you continue on your journey to become an exemplary follower.

First, the organization must develop a context for developing effective teams.[10] This means managers are more likely to achieve successful team dynamics. Within the context of team building within an organization, the type of team needed must be determined. Dyer, Dyer, and Dyer indicate there are three types of teams: decision teams, task teams, and self-directed teams. The first two types are self-explanatory but a self-directed team is an autonomous team without a designated leader. Without this proper context within the organization to support team work it will be very difficult to develop teams. Therefore, it is important for you to learn team building skills.

Now that the context of teamwork has been established, and there is a culture of team building and team performance in the organization, the next requirement is to answer the question about the composition of the team.[11] In other words, who should be on the team? The team members must have the experience and skills to accomplish the task at hand whatever it may be.

The experience and skill of the individual team members is of utmost importance as these skills can eventually develop into team competencies.[12] These team competencies should be nurtured and shared with all individual members of the team. One way this development can take place is by shifting from management to leadership. Remember the adage that you manage things and lead people. The team is made up of people and they will need leadership. This leadership can come from several sources; the designated leader is not the only team member capable of leading.

The final C is associated with change.[13] Change is inevitable when working with teams. As an exemplary follower, you may be called upon to help implement change within the context and competencies of the team. Therefore, your goal as an exemplary follower or team member is to help the team become aware of the situations within the team that keeps it from functioning properly.[14]

The reason I put this book together is to share with you what I have learned from over 40 years of work experience about leadership and followership, and Euclid was correct. We began by sharing information about leadership theories (most you were familiar with) and followership theories (probably not so familiar). After these two foundation chapters, we discussed how to prepare for the job you have right now and the one you would like to have next. Remember it is important to make your boss's job easy. Next we discussed how to gain an understanding of what is required of you in any job that you may have, now or in the future. We then touched on the need for good communication, the display of initiative, and the need for maintaining a positive mental attitude. Next a discussion of what it means to accept responsibility for the things you can control. Finally, we wrapped up with a few words about problem solving and teamwork. Both are very important to an exemplary follower.

After you have read this book, one thing should be abundantly clear is that it all comes down to you and your definition of success. Take a few minutes and give some thought to what success means to you in your chosen career path. And keep in mind that these important skills will serve you regardless of the job or position you have, as everyone has a boss, and we all work for someone. Even if you are the boss, you work for someone and someone works for you and these are the skills that you and your employees should learn. Keep in mind that true principles are true regardless of the circumstances. The more experience you have with true principles and the more exposure you have to true principles the better able you are to pick and choose in order to refine and sharpen your skills as an exemplary follower. There is no one correct way to lead or follow, but you should make your way an excellent way. Be as good as you can be in the situation you find yourself in right now.

About the Author

James H. Schindler grew up in Kansas. After an enlistment in the USAF, he graduated from the University of South Alabama with a BS in Biology and Chemistry. After graduation, he went to the USAF Officer Training School and had a successful career with many assignments worldwide. Before leaving the USAF, he served at Maxwell AFB, AL, teaching at the Air University where he taught leadership and communication skills. While on active duty, he earned his MS in personnel management from Troy University Montgomery. He went on to earn a DBA degree with a concentration in leadership from Walden University.

Dr. Schindler is a professor of business administration at Columbia Southern University where he teaches both graduate and undergraduate courses. Dr. Schindler lives with his wife Ruthann in Magnolia Springs, Alabama; he has five grown children and 11 grandchildren. His wife has five grown children and nine grandchildren.

Notes

Chapter 1

1. Kelley (1992).
2. Dixon and Westbrook (2003).
3. Bjugstad et al. (2006).
4. Agho (2009).
5. Chaleff (2003).
6. Chaleff (2003).
7. Carlyle (1888).
8. Cherry (2014). "Gordon Allport Biography."
9. Cherry (2014). "Raymond Cattell Biography (1905–1998)."
10. Center (2014).
11. Fiske (1949).
12. Norman (1967).
13. Goldberg (1981).
14. McCrae and Costa (1996).
15. Tupes and Christal (1961).
16. Seyranian (2009).
17. Seyranian (2009).
18. Seyranian (2009).
19. Seyranian (2009).
20. Seyranian (2009).
21. Seyranian (2009).
22. Seyranian (2009).
23. "Behavioral Theories of Leadership" (2013).
24. "Behavioral Theories of Leadership" (2013).
25. "Transactional Leadership Theory" (2014).
26. Scribd (2014).
27. "Transactional Leadership Theory" (2014).
28. Cherry (2014). "Leadership Theories - 8 Major Leadership Theories."
29. Cherry (2014). "Leadership Theories - 8 Major Leadership Theories."
30. Cherry (2014). "Leadership Theories - 8 Major Leadership Theories."
31. Heath (1908).

Chapter 2

1. Bennis and Nanus (1985).
2. Blackshear (2004).
3. Blackshear (2004).
4. Agho (2009).
5. Kelley (1988).
6. Chaleff (2003).
7. Dixon (2009).
8. Kelley (1988).
9. Kelley (2008).
10. Kelley (2008).
11. Kelley (2008).
12. Chaleff (2003).
13. Chaleff (2003).
14. Chaleff (2003).
15. Latour and Rast (2004).
16. Blackshear (2004).
17. Blackshear (2004).
18. Mellinger (2012).
19. Mellinger (2012).
20. Bossidy (2008).

Chapter 3

1. Heath (1908).
2. Canter (2006).
3. Canter (2006).
4. Freedman (2007).
5. Freedman (2007).
6. "Competent" (2013). In *Dictionary.com*.
7. Sandberg (2000).
8. Braniac (2014).
9. Pinder (2008).
10. McClelland (1965).
11. Jex and Britt (2008).
12. "Your #1 Job is to Make Your Boss's Life Easier" (2011).
13. Jex and Britt (2008).
14. Jex and Britt (2008).
15. Jex and Britt (2008).
16. Jex and Britt (2008).
17. Jex and Britt (2008).

18. Jex and Britt (2008).
19. Bell and Smith (2003).

Chapter 4

1. Conhan (2014).
2. "10 Ways to Meet and Exceed Your Boss's Expectations" (2014).
3. "10 Ways to Meet and Exceed Your Boss's Expectations" (2014).
4. Chaleff (2003).
5. Chaleff (2003).
6. "Building a Productive Relationship with Your Manager" (2013).
7. "Building a Productive Relationship with Your Manager" (2013).
8. "Building a Productive Relationship with Your Manager" (2013).
9. "Building a Productive Relationship with Your Manager" (2013).
10. "Building a Productive Relationship with Your Manager" (2013).
11. "Building a Productive Relationship with Your Manager" (2013).
12. "Building a Productive Relationship with Your Manager" (2013).
13. McQuerrey (2014).
14. McQuerrey (2014).
15. McQuerrey (2014).
16. McQuerrey (2014).
17. "Being Honest" (2013).

Chapter 5

1. AFH 37-137 (1994).
2. AFH 37-137 (1994).
3. DuBrin (2009).
4. "The 7 Cs of Communication: A Checklist for Clear Communication" (2014).
5. "The 7 Cs of Communication: A Checklist for Clear Communication" (2014).
6. Bilanich (2009).

Chapter 6

1. "Imagination [Def. 1]" (2013). In *Merriam-Webster Online*.
2. "From Imagination to Realization – Bridging the Gap" (2014).
3. Angier (2014).
4. Angier (2014).
5. Nadia (2013).
6. Nadia (2013).
7. Nadia (2013).

8. Nadia (2013).
9. Nadia (2013).

Chapter 7

1. James (2013).
2. Tracey (2013).
3. James (2013).
4. James (2013).
5. James (2013).
6. James (2013).
7. James (2013).
8. O'Flaherty (2014).
9. O'Flaherty (2014).
10. O'Flaherty (2014).
11. O'Flaherty (2014).
12. O'Flaherty (2014).
13. O'Flaherty (2014).
14. O'Flaherty (2014).
15. Covey (2004).
16. Thomassian (2012).
17. Thomassian (2012).
18. Thomassian (2012).
19. Thomassian (2012).
20. Thomassian (2012).
21. Thomassian (2012).
22. Thomassian (2012).
23. Su (2010).
24. Su (2010).
25. Su (2010).
26. Su (2010).
27. Su (2010).
28. Su (2010).

Chapter 8

1. Beaumont (2005).
2. Beaumont (2005).
3. Beaumont (2005).
4. "Being Honest" (2013).
5. Ross (2012).
6. Josephson (2011).

7. Mikey (2013).
8. Haskins (2009).
9. Haskins (2009).
10. Mikey (2013).
11. Mikey (2013).
12. Mikey (2013).
13. Mikey (2013).
14. Mikey (2013).
15. Mikey (2013).
16. Mikey (2013).
17. Mikey (2013).

Chapter 9

1. "Problem Solving and Analytical Skills" (2013).
2. "Problem Solving and Analytical Skills" (2013).
3. "Problem Solving and Analytical Skills" (2013).
4. "Problem Solving and Analytical Skills" (2013).
5. Cherry (2014). "Problem Solving: Problem Solving Strategies and Obstacles."
6. Cherry (2014). "Problem Solving: Problem Solving Strategies and Obstacles."
7. Cherry (2014). "Problem Solving: Problem Solving Strategies and Obstacles."
8. Cherry (2014). "Problem Solving: Problem Solving Strategies and Obstacles."
9. Cherry (2014). "Problem Solving: Problem Solving Strategies and Obstacles."
10. Cherry (2014). "Problem Solving: Problem Solving Strategies and Obstacles."

Chapter 10

1. "8 Steps to Improve Teamwork Skills" (2013).
2. "8 Steps to Improve Teamwork Skills" (2013).
3. "8 Steps to Improve Teamwork Skills" (2013).
4. "8 Steps to Improve Teamwork Skills" (2013).
5. "8 Steps to Improve Teamwork Skills" (2013).
6. "8 Steps to Improve Teamwork Skills" (2013).
7. "8 Steps to Improve Teamwork Skills" (2013).
8. "8 Steps to Improve Teamwork Skills" (2013).
9. Dyer, W.G., W.G. Dyer Jr., and J.H. Dyer (2007).
10. Dyer, W.G., W.G. Dyer Jr., and J.H. Dyer (2007).
11. Dyer, W.G., W.G. Dyer Jr., and J.H. Dyer (2007).
12. Dyer, W.G., W.G. Dyer Jr., and J.H. Dyer (2007).
13. Dyer, W.G., W.G. Dyer Jr., and J.H. Dyer (2007).
14. Dyer, W.G., W.G. Dyer Jr., and J.H. Dyer (2007).

References

"10 Ways to Meet and Exceed Your Boss's Expectations." 2014. KForce. http://www.kforce.com/Career-Resources/10-Ways-to-Meet-and-Exceed-Your-Boss-Expectations.aspx

"8 Steps to Improve Teamwork Skills." 2013. Smart Blog. http://jonny-smartblog.blogspot.com/2012/06/8-steps-to-improve-teamwork-skills.html

AFH 37–137. 1994. *The Tongue and Quill: Communicating Is a Powerful Tool for the Twenty-First Century Air Force.* Washington, DC: Secretary of the Air Force.

Agho, A.O. 2009. "Perspectives of Senior-Level Executives on Effective Followership and Leadership." *Journal of Leadership & Organizational Studies* 16, no. 2, pp. 159–66. doi:10.1177/1548051809335360

Angier, M. 2007. "Top Ten Ways to Inspire Others to be Their Best." *Appleseeds.* http://www.appleseeds.org/10-inspire_Angier.htm

Beaumont, L.R. 2005. "Responsibility: My role." Emotional Competency. http://www.emotionalcompetency.com/responsibility.htm

"Behavioral Theories of Leadership." 2013. Techno Func. http://www.technofunc.com/index.php/leadership-skills/leadership-theories/item/behavioral-theories-of-leadership

"Being Honest." 2013. Vital Life Affirmations. http://www.vitalaffirmations.com/being-honest.htm#.UcihHtiSL2Q

Bell, A.H., and D.M. Smith. 2003. *Motivating Yourself for Achievement.* Upper Saddle River, NJ: Prentice Hall.

Bennis, W., and B. Nanus. 1985. *Leaders: The Strategies for Taking Charge.* New York: Harper and Row.

Bilanich, B. 2009. "Choose Your Words Carefully for Success." Fast Company. http://www.fastcompany.com/1208534/choose-your-words-carefully-success

Bjugstad, K., E.C. Thach, K.J. Thompson, and A. Morris. 2006. "A Fresh Look at Followership: A Model for Matching Followership and Leadership Styles." *Journal of Behavioral and Applied Management* 7, pp. 304–319, http://www.ibam.com/pubs/jbam/default.asp

Blackshear, P.B. 2004. "The Followership Continuum: A Model for Increasing Organizational Productivity." *The Innovation Journal* 9, no. 1.

Bossidy, L. 2008. "What Your Leader Expects of You." *Leadership Excellence* 25, no. 2, p. 6.

Braniac. 2014. "How to Prepare for Your Career Future." eHow. http://www.ehow.com/how_2343816_prepare-career-future.html

"Building a Productive Relationship with Your Manager." 2013. Life Works. https:// portal.lifeworks.com/portal/Viewers/HPSArticle.aspx?HPSMaterial ID=14439

Canter, R.J. 2006. *Make the Right Career Move: 28 Critical Insights and Strategies to Land Your Dream Job.* New York: John Wiley & Sons Publishing.

Carlyle, T. 1888. *On Heroes, Hero Worship and the Heroic in History.* New York: Fredrick A. Stokes & Brothers.

Center, D. 2009. "The Three Factor Theory of Personality." http://www.davidcenter.com/documents/Journal%20Articles/45.pdf

Chaleff, I. 2003. *The courageous follower: Standing up to & for our leaders.* 2nd ed. San Francisco, CA: Barrett-Koehler Publishers ,Inc.

Cherry, K. 2014. "Gordon Allport Biography." About.com: Psychology. http:// psychology.about.com/od/profilesal/p/gordon-allport.htm

Cherry, K. 2014. "Leadership Theories - 8 Major Leadership Theories." About.com: Psychology. http://psychology.about.com/od/leadership/p/leadtheories.htm

Cherry, K. 2014. "Problem Solving: Problem Solving Strategies and Obstacles." About.com: Psychology. psychology.about.com/od/cognitivepsychology/a/problemsolving.htm

Cherry, K. 2014. "Raymond Cattell Biography (1905-1998)." About.com: Psychology. http://psychology.about.com/od/profilesal/p/raymond-cattell.htm

"Competent." 2013. Dictionary.com. http://dictionary.reference.com/ (accessed on June 19).

Conhan, C. 2014. "5 Questions You Need to Ask Your Boss Today." Monster. http://career-advice.monster.com/in-the-office/workplace-issues/questions-to-ask-boss/article.aspx

Covey, S. 2004. *The 7 Habits of Highly Effective People.* New York: Simon and Shuster.

Dixon, G. 2009. "Can We Lead and Follow?" *Engineering Management Journal* 21, pp. 34–41. https://netforum.avectra.com/eweb/DynamicPage.aspx?Site=asem&WebCode=EMJ

Dixon, G., and J. Westbrook. 2003. "Followers Revealed." *Engineering Management Journal* 15, pp. 19–25. https://netforum.avectra.com/eweb/DynamicPage.aspx?Site=asem&WebCode=EMJ

DuBrin, A.J. 2009. *Human Relations: Interpersonal Job-Oriented Skills.* 6th ed. Upper Saddle River, NJ: Prentice Hall.

Dyer, W.G., W.G. Dyer Jr., and J.H. Dyer. 2007. *Team Building: Proven Strategies for Improving Team Performance.* 4th ed. San Francisco, CA: Jossey-Bass.

Fiske, D.W. 1949. "Consistency of the Factorial Structures of Personality Ratings from Different Sources." *Journal of Abnormal Social Psychology* 44, no. 3, pp. 329–44.

Freedman, E. 2007. *Work 101: Learning the Ropes of the Workplace Without Hanging Yourself.* McHenry, IL: Delta Publishing.

"From Imagination to Realization – Bridging the Gap." 2014. Advanced Life Skills. http://advancedlifeskills.com/blog/from-imagination-to-realization-bridging-the-gap/

Goldberg, L.R. 1981. "Language and Individual Differences: The Search for Universals in Personality Lexicons." In Vol. 2 of Review of Personality and Social Psychology, ed. L. Wheeler, 141–65. Beverly Hills, CA: Sage.

Haskins, R. 2009. "The Sequence of Personal Responsibility." Brookings. http://www.brookings.edu/research/articles/2009/07/09-responsibility-haskins

Heath, T.L. 1908. The Thirteen Books of Euclid's Elements. Reprint, New York: Dover Publications, 1956.

"Imagination [Def. 1]." 2013. Merriam-Webster Online. http://www.merriam-webster.com/dictionary/imagination (accessed on August 29).

James, G. 2013. "How to Create a Positive Attitude." Inc. http://www.inc.com/geoffrey-james/how-to-create-a-positive-attitude.html

Jex, S.M., and T.W. Britt. 2008. Organizational Psychology. Hoboken, NJ: John Wiley & Sons Inc.

Josephson, M. 2011. "Trustworthiness and Integrity: What It Takes and Why Its So Hard." Josephson Institute. http://josephsoninstitute.org/business/blog/2011/01/trustworthiness-and-integrity-what-it-takes-and-whyit%E2%80%99s-so-hard

Kelley, R. 1992. The Power of Followership. New York: Currency, Doubleday.

Kelley, R.E. 1988. "In Praise of Followers." Harvard Business Review 66, no. 6, pp. 142–8.

Kelley, R.E. 2008. "Rethinking Followership." In The Art of Followership: How Great Followers Create Great Leaders and Organizations, eds. R.R. Riggio, I.C. Chaleff, and J. Lipman-Blumen, 5–15. San Francisco, CA: Jossey-Bass.

Latour, S.M., and V.J. Rast. 2004. "Dynamic Followership: The Prerequisite for Effective Leadership." Air & Space Power Journal 18, no. 4.

McClelland, D. 1965. "Toward A Theory of Motive Acquisition." American Psychologist 20, no. 5, pp. 321–33.

McCrae, R.R., and P.T. Costa. 1996. "Toward a New Generation of Personality Theories: Theoretical Contexts for the Five Factor Model." In The Five Factor Model of Personality, ed. J. Wiggens. New York: Guilford Press.

McQuerrey, L. 2014. "How to Show Loyalty to the Boss." Global Post. http://everydaylife.globalpost.com/show-loyalty-boss-10757.html

Mellinger, P.S. 2012. "The Ten Rules of Good Followership." In AU-24, Concepts for Air Force Leadership

Mikey, D. 2013. "Take Personal Responsibility for Your Life and Your Happiness." Feel Happiness. http://feelhappiness.com/take-personal-responsibility-for-your-happiness/

Nadia, G. 2013. "How To Break the Mold and be an Independent Thinker." Entrepreneur. http://www.entrepreneur.com/article/227239

Norman, W.T. 1967. *2,800 Personality Trait Descriptors: Normative Operating Characteristics for a University Population*. Ann Arbor, MI: Department of Psychology, University of Michigan

O'Flaherty, D. 2014. "8 Tips to Help Create a Positive Mental Attitude." Tiny Buddha. http://tinybuddha.com/blog/8-tips-to-help-create-a-positive-mental-attitude/

Pinder, C.C. 2008. *Work Motivation in Organizational Behavior*. 2nd ed. New York: Psychology Press.

"Problem Solving and Analytical Skills." 2013. University of Kent. http://www.kent.ac.uk/careers/sk/problem-solving-skills.htm

River Crossing Puzzles. 2014. BrainDen. http://brainden.com/crossing-river.htm

Ross D. 2012. "Can You Develop Integrity?" Results Through Integrity. http://www.resultsthroughintegrity.com/resultsthroughintegrity/personal_stories_of_integrity/

Sandberg, J. 2000. "Understanding Human Competence at Work: An Interpretive Approach." *Academy of Management Journal* 43, no. 1, pp. 9–45, http://www.expertisecentrumlerenvandocenten.nl/files/sandberg.pdf

Scribd. 2014. "Transactional Leadership Theory." http://www.scribd.com/doc/59528298/Transactional-Leadership-Theory

Seyranian, V. "Contingency Theories of Leadership." In *Encyclopedia of Group Processes & Intergroup Relations*, ed. J.M. Levine and M.A. Hogg, 152–56. Thousand Oaks, CA: SAGE, 2009. SAGE Reference Online. Web. 30 Jan. 2012

Su, T. 2010. "The 5 Myths of Positive Mental Attitude." Think Simple Now. http://thinksimplenow.com/happiness/the-5-myths-of-positive-mental-attitude/

"The 7 Cs of Communication: A Checklist for Clear Communication." 2014. Mind Tools. http://www.mindtools.com/pages/article/newCS_85.htm

Thomassian, M. 2012. "7 Strategies to Developing a Positive Mental Attitude." http://www.stevenaitchison.co.uk/blog/7-strategiesto-developing-a-positive-mental-attitude/

Tracey, B. 2013. "Dream Big: Live your Life without Limits." Brian Tracy's Blog. http://www.briantracy.com/blog/personal-success/dream-big-live-your-lifewithout-limits/#ixzz2nxJvZj8g

"Transactional Leadership Theory." 2014. Management Study Guide. http://www.managementstudyguide.com/transactional-leadership.htm

Tupes, E.C., and R.E. Christal. 1961. Recurrent Personality Factors Based on Trait Ratings. Technical Report ASD-TR-61-97, Lackland Air Force Base. San Antonio, TX: Personnel Laboratory, Air Force Systems Command.

"Your #1 Job is to Make Your Boss's Life Easier." 2011. Manager Cheat Sheet. http://managercheatsheet.com/2011/02/02/your-1-job-is-to-make-your-bosss-life-easier/

Index

OTHER TITLES IN THE HUMAN RESOURCE MANAGEMENT AND ORGANIZATIONAL BEHAVIOR COLLECTION
Jean Phillips and Stan Gully, Rutgers University, Editors

- *Culturally Intelligent Leadership: Leading Through Intercultural Interactions* by Mai Moua
- *Letting People Go: The People-Centered Approach to Firing and Laying Off Employees* by Matt Shlosberg
- *The Five Golden Rules of Negotiation* by Philippe Korda
- *Cross-Cultural Management* by Veronica Velo
- *Conversations About Job Performance: A Communication Perspective on the Appraisal Process* by Michael E. Gordon and Vernon Miller
- *How to Coach Individuals, Teams, and Organizations to Master Transformational Change: Surfing Tsunamis* by Stephen K. Hacker
- *Managing Employee Turnover: Dispelling Myths and Fostering Evidence-Based Retention Strategies* by David Allen and Phil Bryant
- *Effective Interviewing and Information Gathering: Proven Tactics to Improve Your Questioning Skills* by Thomas Diamante
- *Developing Employee Talent to Perform: People Power* by Kim Warren
- *Fostering Creativity in Self and the Organization: Your Professional Edge* by Eric W. Stein
- *Designing Creative High Power Teams and Organizations: Beyond Leadership* by Eric W. Stein
- *Creating a Pathway to Your Dream Career: Designing and Controlling a Career Around Your Life Goals* by Tom Kucharvy
- *Leader Evolution: From Technical Expertise to Strategic Leadership* by Alan Patterson

Announcing the Business Expert Press Digital Library
Concise e-books business students need for classroom and research

This book can also be purchased in an e-book collection by your library as

- a one-time purchase,
- that is owned forever,
- allows for simultaneous readers,
- has no restrictions on printing, and
- can be downloaded as PDFs from within the library community.

Our digital library collections are a great solution to beat the rising cost of textbooks. E-books can be loaded into their course management systems or onto students' e-book readers.
The **Business Expert Press** digital libraries are very affordable, with no obligation to buy in future years. For more information, please visit **www.businessexpertpress.com/librarians**. To set up a trial in the United States, please email **sales@businessexpertpress.com**.